Practical Guide to SAP® Profit Center Accounting

John Pringle

Thank you for purchasing this book from Espresso Tutorials!

Like a cup of espresso coffee, Espresso Tutorials SAP books are concise and effective. We know that your time is valuable and we deliver information in a succinct and straightforward manner. It only takes our readers a short amount of time to consume SAP concepts. Our books are well recognized in the industry for leveraging tutorial-style instruction and videos to show you step by step how to successfully work with SAP.

Check out our YouTube channel to watch our videos at
https://www.youtube.com/user/EspressoTutorials.

If you are interested in SAP Finance and Controlling, join us at
http://www.fico-forum.com/forum2/
to get your SAP questions answered and contribute to discussions.

Related titles from Espresso Tutorials:

- ▶ Martin Munzel: New SAP® Controlling Planning Interface
  http://5011.espresso-tutorials.com
- ▶ Michael Esser: Investment Project Controlling with SAP®
  http://5008.espresso-tutorials.com
- ▶ Stefan Eifler: Quick Guide to SAP® CO-PA (Profitability Analysis) http://5018.espresso-tutorials.com
- ▶ Paul Ovigele: Reconciling SAP® CO-PA to the General Ledger
  http://5040.espresso-tutorials.com
- ▶ Tanya Duncan: Practical Guide to SAP® CO-PC (Product Cost Controlling)
  http://5064.espresso-tutorials.com
- ▶ Ashish Sampat: First Steps in SAP® Controlling (CO)
  http://5069.espresso-tutorials.com
- ▶ Rosana Fonseca: Practical Guide to SAP® Material Ledger (ML)
  http://5116.espresso-tutorials.com

All you can read:
The SAP eBook Library
http://free.espresso-tutorials.com

- Annual online subscription
- SAP information at your fingertips
- Free 30-day trial

John Pringle
Practical Guide to SAP® Profit Center Accounting

ISBN:	978-1-5353-0539-6
Editor:	Lisa Jackson
Cover Design:	Philip Esch, Martin Munzel
Cover Photo:	Fotolia #80633004 airdone
Interior Design:	Johann-Christian Hanke

All rights reserved.

1st Edition 2016, Gleichen

© 2016 by Espresso Tutorials GmbH

URL: *www.espresso-tutorials.com*

All rights reserved. Neither this publication nor any part of it may be copied or reproduced in any form or by any means or translated into another language without the prior consent of Espresso Tutorials GmbH, Zum Gelenberg 11, 37130 Gleichen, Germany.

Espresso Tutorials makes no warranties or representations with respects to the content hereof and specifically disclaims any implied warranties of merchantability or fitness for any particular purpose. Espresso Tutorials assumes no responsibility for any errors that may appear in this publication.

Feedback
We greatly appreciate any kind of feedback you have concerning this book. Please mail us at *info@espresso-tutorials.com*.

Table of Contents

Preface   **7**

1 Introduction to profit center accounting   **11**
- 1.1 Business requirements for profitability management and reporting   11
- 1.2 PCA versus COPA   12
- 1.3 Evolution of profit center accounting   17
- 1.4 Summary   20

2 Master data in PCA   **21**
- 2.1 Profit center   21
- 2.2 The dummy profit center   30
- 2.3 Profit center standard hierarchy   31
- 2.4 Profit center group   34
- 2.5 Revenue/cost elements and accounts   37
- 2.6 Account groups   38
- 2.7 Statistical key figures   39
- 2.8 Profit center assignment   43
- 2.9 Summary   55

3 Planning in classic PCA   **57**
- 3.1 How profit center planning fits   57
- 3.2 Planning version concept in SAP   59
- 3.3 Integrated revenue and COGS planning   60
- 3.4 Integrated cost planning   64
- 3.5 Statistical key figure planning   71
- 3.6 Manual planning in classic PCA   73
- 3.7 Summary   87

4 Profit center planning in the new GL   **89**
- 4.1 How new GL planning fits   89

	4.2	Planning version concept in new GL	90
	4.3	Integrated revenue and COGS planning	92
	4.4	Integrated cost planning in the new GL	94
	4.5	Statistical key figure planning in the GL	98
	4.6	Manual planning in the new GL	98
	4.7	Summary	107
5	**Profit center actual postings**		**109**
	5.1	Flow of actual values in classic PCA	109
	5.2	Manual posting in classic PCA	121
	5.3	Flow of actual values in the new GL	123
	5.4	Actual statistical key figures	132
	5.5	Periodic processes	136
	5.6	Summary	136
6	**Profit center transfer pricing**		**137**
	6.1	Transfer pricing scenarios in SAP	137
	6.2	Transfer pricing setup	138
	6.3	Transfer pricing in practice	146
	6.4	Summary	150
7	**Reporting in profit center accounting**		**151**
	7.1	Reporting in classic PCA	151
	7.2	Profit center reporting in the new GL	161
	7.3	Report painter and drilldown options	165
	7.4	Summary	173
A	**The Author**		**176**
B	**Index**		**177**
C	**Disclaimer**		**180**

Preface

Although many of my more logistic-minded colleagues will not appreciate me saying so, the ultimate measure of a business's success is generally measured in financial terms. I have been involved in ERP (enterprise resource planning) implementation projects for almost twenty years and I have yet to see a project where core financial modules are excluded or even deferred to a later project phase (I don't even think it is really possible). In most ERP systems I have seen, and in SAP in particular, all roads eventually lead to finance. There will always be a need to track and report upon the financial impacts of the business activities within the organization. This requirement has not changed since Luca Pacioli first documented double-entry bookkeeping for Venetian merchants in the 15th century. The only thing that has changed and is still changing is our ability to access, analyze, and report on the results in faster and faster ways. We have gone from ledger books and written records to computerized accounting systems to ERP systems to data warehouses and advanced analytics. The goal of this advancement is primarily to accommodate higher volumes of transactions and to give businesses faster and better insights into their financial results and, in particular, their profitability.

In SAP ECC, this ability to report and analyze profitability resides in three different places: the general ledger (GL), profit center accounting (PCA), and profitability analysis (COPA). This book is intended to focus on the area of profit center accounting within SAP and also to some extent the general ledger. There are actually two different profit center accountings in SAP and this book will explain the difference between the two approaches and why you might be using one rather than the other. After explaining what profit center accounting is in SAP and what data objects are linked to it, I focus on the basic business functions, namely planning, actual postings, and reporting.

Throughout the book it may become easy to get lost in the individual functional transactions within profit center accounting, but it is important to keep in mind that the overall goal is to set profitability targets for business (planning) and then compare actual results against those targets. Everything shown in this book is to meet this goal. To this end, the book is divided logically into sections, each dealing with one of the primary functions of the module. Over the course of two chapters, you will look at planning in some detail. You will focus on how you can get your planning data into the module. Then you will examine how the actual results come into profit center accounting and are compared against the plan values. You will also look at an additional functionality within SAP which can have a considerable impact on profit center accounting; this is called transfer pricing. The nature of this subject requires a chapter dealing largely with setup and configuration. It may seem overly technical to some readers. Finally, you will learn some of the reporting options that will allow you to compare your planned data versus your actual results, including some options for creating your own reports.

Whether you are planning to implement SAP or are already live with either the classic PCA approach or the new GL approach, you will find this book useful to help you understand PCA and ensure that you are getting the most out of your PCA module.

Acknowledgements

This book is dedicated to my wife, Lynn, and my, children Ness and John. I also want to thank Martin Munzel and Alice Adams of Espresso Tutorials for approaching me and suggesting that I might like to write a book (good call guys). It has been a wonderful experience working with such professional people. Finally, thanks to my consulting and support colleagues at Illumiti who always keep me on my toes and to our clients who always seem to come up with different business requirements to ensure that I am never bored in my work.

We have added a few icons to highlight important information. These include:

Tips

Tips highlight information concerning more details about the subject being described and/or additional background information.

Attention

Attention notices draw attention to information that you should be aware of when you go through the examples from this book on your own.

Finally, a note concerning the copyright: all screenshots printed in this book are the copyright of SAP SE. All rights are reserved by SAP SE. Copyright pertains to all SAP images in this publication. For simplification, we will not mention this specifically underneath every screenshot.

1 Introduction to profit center accounting

In this chapter, I address the business requirements for understanding profitability and how these can be met in SAP. I explain the basic differences between profit center accounting (PCA) and controlling profitability analysis (COPA) and suggest scenarios where each may be used. I also explain a little of the evolution of PCA within SAP, specifically the changes that came about with the introduction of the new GL in SAP ECC release 5.0 in 2004.

1.1 Business requirements for profitability management and reporting

As I stated in the introduction, the primary goal of any business venture should be to achieve and maintain profitability. From an IT perspective, businesses require the tools to report and analyze past and current profitability results, as well as to plan and forecast future results.

Within SAP ECC, there are several tools available to report and plan profitability. At the company code level, there are various financial statement reporting options using an income statement based on a financial statement version to report on periodic profitability at a legal entity basis. This provides a one-dimensional view of profitability at the company code level. However, this is rather limited and many businesses would like to see and plan their profitability based on dimensions other than the legal entity or company code. To this end, SAP provides two other tools or modules to allow the business to report and plan profitability. The first of these is profit center accounting EC-PCA which is the primary subject of this book; the second is profitability analysis, commonly known as COPA. By way of explanation the EC prefix is a reference to a module in SAP called enterprise controlling which contains functionality for executive information systems (EIS), planning, and consolidations in addition to profit center accounting. Other than PCA, the functions in enterprise consolidation are no longer supported by SAP and have been superseded by other tools such as business planning and consolidations (BPC) and various reporting options in business objects (BOBJ) and business warehouse (BW). The EC prefix is still seen in some SAP documentation for

PCA, but for the rest of this book only the acronym PCA will be used. In the next section, I explain the basic difference between these two modules and when it is appropriate to use each.

1.2 PCA versus COPA

It may appear, based on the title of this section that I am setting PCA against COPA in a "one or the other" type of scenario. This is not really the case; both of these modules can co-exist quite happily in your SAP system. However, it is important to understand what each of the modules brings to the table in terms of functionality and where they can fit within your reporting and planning framework. The decision on whether to use one or both of these modules will be dependent on the profitability accounting requirements within your organization.

The best way to compare the two modules is to look at how SAP positions them based on their business purpose and structure.

The business purpose and structure of profit center accounting is to:

- Provide profitability information based on the physical or management structure of the business
- Provide information and allow planning based on responsibility area such as region, business function, or product
- Use a structure defined in terms of profit centers and arranged in a *standard hierarchy*
- Post values using accounts
- Easily achieve a full profit and loss (P&L) statement by profit center
- Assign balance sheet items to profit centers, allowing calculation of financial ratios, such as return on investment

The business purpose and structure of profitability analysis is to:

- Provide profitability information based on flexible criteria such as market segment
- Generally support decision making, often in the sales and marketing area
- Use a structure based on groupings of characteristics from the customer, material, and selling organizations

- Post values using accounts (account based) and/or value fields (costing based)
- Easily achieve gross margin level reports by market segment
- Balance sheet items are not posted to COPA

The key thing to understand about both PCA and COPA is that they are, what I call, *downstream modules*. In general, actual data flows into them from other modules in SAP. It is usually not advisable, and in some cases not possible, to make actual postings in these modules and if you do, these postings will not flow back to the source modules.

Actual posting data will flow in real time into PCA from financial transactions. These may be automatically generated financial transactions coming, for example, from logistic or production activity, or they may just be direct financial postings entered through *financial accounting* (FI). This will be the case regardless of whether you are using classic PCA or PCA in the new GL. The mechanics and timing of how this happens may vary between the two, but the end result is essentially the same.

The actual posting data flow into costing-based COPA is somewhat different. Since the profitability segment in COPA is itself a real cost object like a cost center or an order, it is not possible for COPA to get many of the postings in real time in the same way that PCA does. Instead, COPA gets real-time postings from sales activities, generally from the billing document. These are usually the sales revenue and sales deduction items reflected in pricing conditions in the sales document. Also, at this time, COPA will receive the cost of sales posting, usually based on a cost estimate for the material being sold. This is obtained from product costing. Then, depending on the requirement of the business, COPA will receive periodic postings. These may include settlement of production variances, allocations from other CO objects, and occasionally direct postings from financial accounting.

PCA and COPA also differ in how they handle planning. While you can plan manually to profit centers, either in the classic or new GL version, they really should be integrated to receive plan data from other CO modules. Most commonly, these will be cost center planning, internal order planning, project planning, and COPA planning. In PCA, the final plan data will reflect the responsibility view of the organization that you have determined based on how you have created your profit centers and hierarchies.

In contrast, for COPA planning, values will be visible at the level of profitability segments. These are groupings of the characteristics that were defined in your system when COPA was initially configured. Plan data may be entered based on a particular combination of characteristics and then additional levels of characteristics may be derived based on the entered values.

As an example, you may set up COPA to plan sales quantity by product and customer ship-to. You can then use *valuation* in COPA planning to determine the sales price, discount, and product cost of these products to get a planned margin by product and customer ship-to. COPA planning also uses characteristic derivation in the same way that actual postings allow you to see planned values at any combination of profitability characteristics that can be derived from the original level of planning. If there is a material hierarchy or a customer hierarchy that is mapped to COPA characteristics, you can see the planned values since they are derived from either the product or ship-to value.

As I said before, the determination of how to use PCA, COPA, or both will be driven by the reporting and planning requirements of the business. As you can infer from its structure, COPA is seen to be more flexible than profit center accounting. COPA is often referred to as being multi-dimensional or is represented as being like a cube that can be reshuffled in a variety of ways to present different views of the profitability data. In addition, it is possible to add characteristics to COPA and re-derive the profitability segments at any time. The profitability segments in COPA can represent many views of profitability data, so it is easy to go from seeing profitability by sales office to seeing it by material group or by any combination of characteristics.

On the other hand, reporting in PCA can be seen as a one-dimensional view based on how you defined your profit centers when your SAP system was implemented. As stated before, profit centers will usually be defined based along organizational lines. These lines may be product related or geographically related or based on some other organizational criteria. This decision of what a profit center will represent should be considered carefully at the blueprint stage of your SAP implementation project since it is very difficult to change at a later date. Basically, unlike COPA, once you have defined the nature of your structure, you are pretty much stuck with it. For example, if you defined your profit centers based on responsibility for geographic regions, but later wanted to restructure based on responsibility for product line, it would be difficult.

In general, profit centers or groupings of profit centers are often used in SAP to represent areas within the organization that are responsible for revenues, costs, and sometimes return on investment. Common business terms for these include business unit (BU), strategic business unit (SBU), responsibility area, reporting unit, and investment center.

Examples for when to use COPA and/or PCA:

- A diversified business that either sells or manufactures and sells a variety of products to a number of customers would likely benefit from using both PCA and COPA. The COPA reporting would provide profitability information based on market segments while the profit center accounting reporting would provide information on revenues, costs, and perhaps return on investment based on lines of business.

- A business that has few products and/or customers may not require sales and distribution functionality in SAP and as a result may not require COPA. As an example, consider companies in the gold mining industry. They produce one primary product and perhaps a few additional by-products. They sell to one or two customers only. They do not use product costing, production planning, or sales and distribution in SAP. In this situation, CO-PA is not relevant. The companies may only be interested in profitability and return by mine location. This can be achieved by creating each mine as a profit center in SAP.

- A business with a simple responsibility structure that still requires market-segment-level profitability may only require profitability reporting and planning from COPA.

As you can see, there are a variety of options and decisions to be made in SAP around profitability reporting and planning:

- Do we need PCA, or COPA, or both?
- If we use COPA, do we use costing based, account based, or both?
- Along what lines will we define our profit centers—how will they represent the responsibility structure of our business?
- Will we use classic profit center accounting, or profit center accounting contained in the SAP general ledger, or both?

I have not talked much about this last point, but understanding the difference between "classic" profit center accounting and "new" GL profit center accounting and knowing how PCA is configured in your system is crucial to understanding how PCA is going to behave for you and which transaction codes you will use for certain functions.

One other thing worth noting at this time is that the introduction of new SAP technology, specifically SAP S/4HANA will have considerable impact on the decisions that you will need to make with both PCA and CO-PA. In many cases, it will actually remove some of the decision points. At the time of writing, the most recent release of SAP S/4HANA is edition 1511 and the following items, which I feel are relevant to either PCA or COPA, are based on my understanding of that release:

- When comparing SAP S/4HANA to SAP ERP 6.0 you will find that certain transaction codes and programs have been replaced with newer transactions, programs, or WebDynpro applications. This is true for several profit center reports which are replaced by WebDynpro or Fiori applications.
- As a result of this, certain functions will no longer be available through the old SAP GUI. For an on-premise solution, it is better to use SAP NetWeaver Business Client (NWBC) or, as it is now called, SAP Business Client or access through SAP Fiori apps in an SAP Fiori launchpad.
- New general ledger is mandatory in SAP S/4HANA
- Account-based COPA is the recommended option, but costing based is still supported and may still be useful in some business situations.
- Overhead cost controlling (CO-OM) planning, P&L planning, and profit center planning are now covered by integrated business planning; the traditional planning transactions have been deactivated in SAP ECC.
- If you do not want to use integrated planning, it is possible to reactivate the old CO-OM planning transactions (SAP Note 1956054), but this is not recommend as a long-term solution.
- Even if you reactivate the old CO-OM planning, the former plan integration to GL planning no longer works.
- Current transfer pricing using legal, group, or profit center valuation is not yet supported as of release 1511. A new approach to parallel valuations will be implemented.

This is only a partial list of changes that have been brought about by SAP S/4HANA, but based on the above and based on statements from SAP; the redesign is the most significant change in the software since the introduction of R3. Looking at past history, it is reasonable to expect that the migration of existing customers to SAP S/4HANA will be a prolonged process. It has been over ten years since the introduction of the new GL and I still meet many existing customers who have not migrated from classic GL to new GL. It is reasonable to expect that the same will be true with SAP S/4HANA.

You will now delve into the setup and functionality of PCA as it exists in SAP ERP 6.0. The next section discusses the difference between classic PCA and the new GL PCA before delving more deeply into the module's functionality in the following chapters. It is first necessary to understand how PCA has evolved over time in the SAP landscape.

1.3 Evolution of profit center accounting

The interesting thing about profit center accounting is that since SAP ECC 5.0 and the introduction of the new architecture for financial accounting, PCA can actually exist in two places. Until the introduction of the new GL, profit center accounting existed as part of controlling. This is referred to as classic profit center accounting. Following the introduction of the new general ledger, profit center accounting was moved into the general ledger. This is referred to as new GL profit center accounting.

To understand the differences, it is necessary to look at what PCA was and what it became. Classic PCA is activated by a configuration setting on the controlling area (see Figure 1.1). It is also a statistical accounting component in SAP Controlling. This means that the profit center itself cannot serve as an account assignment object in CO and that PCA will take transaction data posted to a real account assignment object and derive a profit center posting based on it. To achieve this, classic PCA utilizes a separate ledger (8A) and stores the actual and plan line items and totals records in their own database tables GLPCA, GLPCP, and GLPCT.

Controlling Area	5000	Smarter Sisters Games	
Fiscal Year	2007	to	9999

Activate Components	
Cost Centers	1 Component active
☐ AA: Activity Type	
Order Management	1 Component active
Commit. Management	1 Components active
ProfitAnalysis	2 Component active for costing-based Profitability Analysis
Acty-Based Costing	Component Not Active
☑ Profit Center Acctg	
☐ Projects	

Figure 1.1: Controlling area settings activation of classic PCA

The new GL made it possible to incorporate the profit center as part of the structure of the GL by assigning the *scenario* FIN_PCA to a ledger in FI configuration (see Figure 1.2). A scenario defines which fields are updated in the *general ledger view* from the data in the *entry view*. There are a number of predefined scenarios that can be assigned to ledgers, each with its own update fields. The assignment of FIN_PCA means that the profit center and partner profit center fields will get updated in the new GL tables. In a pure new GL scenario where PCA has not been activated in the controlling area, you should not get a PCA document associated with any postings. The only profit center update will be through the accounting document.

Dialog Structure	Ledger	0L	
∨ ☐ Ledgers			
• ☐ Scenarios	Scenarios		
• ☐ Customer Fields	Scenario f...	Long Text	
• ☐ Versions	FIN_CCA	Cost Center Update	
	FIN_PCA	Profit Center Update	
	FIN_SEGM	Segment Reporting	
	FIN_UKV	Cost of Sales Accounting	

Figure 1.2: Assign PCA scenario to a ledger

There are four possible situations that can exist for profit center accounting in an SAP system.

1. The system is still configured for the classic GL or the new GL is used and the FIN_PCA scenario is not assigned to any ledgers. In this situation, only classic PCA is possible.
2. The system is configured for the new GL either with or without document splitting and classic PCA is disabled in the controlling area settings. In this situation, the profit center posting will only update in the GL tables.
3. The system is configured for the new GL without document splitting and classic PCA is active in the controlling area settings. In this situation, both the GL tables and the profit center tables will be updated by a profit center posting.
4. The system is configured for the new GL with document splitting at the profit center or segment level and classic PCA is active in the controlling area settings. In this situation, both the GL tables and the profit center tables will be updated by a profit center posting. In addition, in the GL, the posting will be split based on profit center or segment, where applicable.

In most of the SAP-provided documentation about setting up the new GL, the recommendation is to use the profit center scenario in the GL and not activate PCA in controlling. Furthermore, it is recommended not to run the two options in parallel. The major concern around this seems to be increased data volume.

The most specific guidance provided by SAP on the topic is provided in SAP note 826357. Here, SAP makes recommendations for new customers and those migrating from the classic GL. For new customers, SAP recommends using the FIN_PCA scenario in the GL and not activating classic PCA in controlling. If full or partial balance sheets are required by profit center, then the use of document splitting by profit center is advocated.

For the migration scenario, SAP states that you can continue to use classic PCA in parallel with the profit center scenario in the new GL, but only recommends this as an interim measure. SAP further recommends that if you need to continue to use classic PCA in parallel with the new GL scenario, then you should not activate document splitting for either the profit center or the segment.

In note 1280060, SAP addresses this topic and again recommends only the FIN_PCA option for new customers. However, in this note, SAP advises existing customers to look at the current usage of classic PCA in their system when making the decision about whether to use classic PCA or the PCA scenario in the new GL. SAP advises that if the current usage of profit centers is for a purpose that is closer to FI, then you should use the PCA scenario in the GL, but if you use PCA in a way that is more supportive to controlling, then you should consider staying with classic PCA.

SAP further outlines benefits of the new GL profit center scenario, including:

- ▶ Not having to reconcile PCA with GL as part of a period-end process—homogeneous ledger environment
- ▶ Not having to run period-end processes to transfer payables and receivables to PCA
- ▶ Having the ability to create a full balance sheet at the profit center level
- ▶ Not having separate year-end processes for GL and PCA

So, if you have a new SAP installation, you will likely be planning to implement the most recent version of the software. Whether this means the latest version of SAP ECC or SAP S/4HANA, you will use the new GL functionality and should not activate classic PCA. If you are an existing SAP customer, you probably plan to continue with your existing configuration until it makes business sense for you to migrate. Either way, you can benefit from a more detailed understanding of PCA.

1.4 Summary

In this chapter, you have seen that the basic methods for profitability reporting and planning within SAP are to use profit centers, COPA, or a combination of both. You have learned the basic differences between PCA and COPA in both their purposes and their designs. You have learned how PCA changed in SAP with the advent of the new GL and you have seen the possible PCA scenarios that could co-exist within an SAP system. Most importantly, you have seen under which conditions classic PCA and new GL PCA can co-exist and when they should not.

2 Master data in PCA

One way of classifying data in SAP is to differentiate between items that are considered master data and items that are considered transactional data. In SAP, master data is relatively static data that is usually defined once and is shared throughout the application. Examples include: vendors, customers, materials, general ledger accounts, cost centers, profit centers, etc. This master data is then used in transactional data such as invoices, billing documents, and material movements. In an SAP implementation project, the structure and definition of master data should be thoroughly planned to properly reflect the needs of the business. Careful consideration should be given to such factors as numbering and naming the master data, permitted field values, and the ultimate reporting aims of the business. In this chapter, I show the relevant master data available in profit center accounting.

2.1 Profit center

As discussed in the previous chapter, the structure of the profit centers is meant to define a responsibility reporting view of the organization. Once the master data is defined, the profit centers are arranged in a hierarchy to represent the responsibility structure of the enterprise. During the design of the system, the nature of that responsibility structure should be determined. Along what lines does the business divide itself? Is it on a geographical basis, a functional basis, a product line basis, some other method, or a combination of some of the above?

Technically, the name of this hierarchy is defined first in the configuration settings and assigned to the controlling area before the profit center masters can be created. This is the case for both classic PCA and for PCA in the new GL. In classic PCA, it is also required to create a dummy profit center before you can start using the standard hierarchy. The concepts of dummy profit center and standard hierarchy are discussed more fully in the following sections.

MASTER DATA IN PCA

The creation of the profit center master data is essentially the same regardless of whether you are using classic PCA or new GL PCA. Transaction KE51 is used to create profit centers (see Figure 2.1).

Create Profit Center

Master Data

| Profit Center | 500010 |

Copy from
| Profit Center | | |
| CO Area | 5000 |

Figure 2.1: Create profit center initial screen

Set the controlling area

Often, when entering transactions in the controlling module in SAP, you are presented with a preliminary screen asking you to enter the controlling area. Having to constantly enter the controlling area can become aggravating, especially when you may only be working with one area. The solution to this is to set your controlling area using transaction OKKS. Enter the controlling area that you work with and press the SAVE button. The value is now stored in your user parameters and remains until you set it to a different value.

It is important before you start creating pieces of master data, such as profit centers, to understand how you are going to name or number them. Unlike some master data objects in SAP, profit center numbering is not driven by a number range object. In fact, it is pretty much free form. You are limited by the field size of up to 10 characters and there are a few special characters such as * that will be rejected; otherwise you can use any alpha-numeric combination you choose. You should also be aware that the profit center, like the cost center, exists in the controlling area, so it is not possible to have a duplicate value within the same controlling area.

Since your profit centers will be tied in some way to other organizational objects in SAP, such as company codes and cost centers, it is prudent to have an overall numbering strategy for these objects before you start creating them in the system. This should reflect the responsibility structure of the organization and be designed to facilitate reporting. Often, the structure or the nature of your business will lead you to a certain strategy in profit center numbering:

- ▶ An organization with a primary focus on manufacturing may be largely concerned with results at a plant level, so may wish to reflect the plant structure somehow in the profit center numbering and hierarchy.
- ▶ An organization with a primary focus on re-selling may be more concerned with results at a regional or product line level so may want to reflect that in the numbering and hierarchy.

In the fictional example, you are setting up profit centers for an organization that manufactures and sells toys and games. They are interested in looking at their results regionally. They operate in four regions; United States, Canada, Europe, and Asia. They are also interested in results by product line. These are: video games, board games, and card games.

Copying master data

Many master data objects will have a COPY FROM or CREATE WITH REFERENCE option to allow you to use an existing piece of master data as a template for your new entry. This can significantly speed up the creation of new pieces of master data.

When you have decided on your profit center number, you can go ahead with transaction KE51 (see Figure 2.2).

The most important information about the profit center is contained on the BASIC DATA tab.

23

Master data in PCA

General Data						
Controlling Area		5000		Smarter Sisters		

Basic Data	Indicators	Company Codes	Address	Communication	History

Descriptions

Profit Center	500010	Status	Inactive: Create
Analysis Period	01.01.2010	to	31.12.9999
Name	Video Games - US		
Long Text	Video Games US Market		

Basic Data

User Responsible	
Person Respons.	Sally Goround
Department	
Profit Ctr Group	5000 Smarter Sisters
Segment	5000

Figure 2.2: Create profit center basic data

The profit center is considered to be a *time-based* object in controlling, which means it is created with a validity period and you can create different data for different time periods. In configuration, certain fields on the master data can be flagged as *time dependent*, resulting in SAP storing a new master record whenever a time-dependent field is changed on a profit center. The ability to create time-based objects is a very important aspect of controlling since it allows you to view master data values at different time periods. For example, the *person responsible* for the profit center may change next year. If *person responsible* is a time-dependent field, then you will have a view of the profit center master when Sally was the person responsible, and then a new view starting when *person responsible* is reassigned.

> **Defining time-dependent fields**
>
>  Since every change to a time-dependent field causes SAP to write a new master record for the data object being changed, you should be very careful in defining fields as time dependent in the system configuration. By defining many time-dependent fields, the data volumes can become large and match-code searches can become confusing for the user, as a piece of master data with more than one time range will appear multiple times in a match-code search. The SAP-delivered configuration should be sufficient for most situations.

The time dependency of the profit center is checked when you create another object with a relationship to it, such as a cost center. If you created your profit center to be valid from 01/01/2015 onwards, you will not be able to create a cost center assigned to that profit center with a valid-from date earlier than 01/01/2015.

> **Valid-from dates and other master data**
>
>  It is best to be aware of other master data requirements when you are setting up validity dates for profit centers, cost centers, and other CO objects. There may be requirements from other modules, such as HR or fixed assets, that the cost centers should exist for a certain time in the past to allow historical data to be loaded. It is good to know that before you create your cost centers and profit centers to avoid a lot of extra rework extending the validity periods after the fact.

Other key fields on the BASIC DATA tab are `person respons`, this is the person responsible for the results of the profit center. There is also `user responsible`, which links to the user master in the SAP system. This field is not mandatory since it is possible that the person responsible for the profit center does not exist as a user in the SAP system. The `department` field is a free text field that can be used to store an external department number. There is no validation on the entry in this field, so the user creating the profit center can enter any value they choose.

The field `profit ctr group` makes the link between the profit center and its place in the standard hierarchy. The *profit center group* selected here is a *node* in the hierarchy. In the initial setup of the profit center structure, there are several different approaches to populating this field. If you are creating other master data, such as material masters which may be dependent on a profit center number, you may want to load or create all the profit centers before you have fully thought out all the levels in the hierarchy. In this case, you may wish to create all the profit centers and assign them to the top hierarchy node and then distribute them later. Alternately, you may have your hierarchy in place and may choose to directly assign each profit center to its correct level during the initial creation.

The final field on the BASIC DATA tab is the segment. The *segment* is an organizational element that was introduced to SAP as part of the new GL. If you have not migrated to the new GL, you will not see the segment as a field in your profit center master and you will not have to worry about it. If you have either migrated to the new GL or have always used new GL, then you will have the segment on your profit center master and you will have considered how the segment is used in your organization.

The segment object was introduced along with other new GL functions, such as parallel ledgers and document splitting, to address evolving accounting standards for both IFRS and US-GAAP. The segment and the document splitting functionality in SAP was aimed towards complying with emerging requirements for segment reporting, which are now defined under IFRS 8 or ASC 280 (US-GAAP). There are still significant differences between US-GAAP and IFRS in the area of segment reporting. For a complete understanding, you should review the relevant accounting guidelines.

For purposes here, it is important to know that SAP designed the segment to be derived from the profit center to which it is assigned. Other enhancements may be made to the system to derive the segment in other ways, but the default is to link the profit center to the segment. The segment can thus be seen as a grouping of profit centers, but the segment will not necessarily fulfill all the functions of a *profit center group*. Instead, the segment should be seen as simply an organizational construct intended to enable the organization to produce balanced financial statements at a level that is different from the company code.

The tracking of segment-level data in the new GL is activated by assigning scenario FIN_SEGM to a ledger in the configuration for financial accounting in the same way that you assigned FIN_PCA. You can refer back to Figure 1.2 to see this. The assignment of the segmentation scenario will result in the update of the segment, partner segment, profit center, and partner profit center.

The segment values themselves are defined in the configuration of the enterprise structure under the definition of financial accounting. The definition of the segment is simply an identifier and a description (see Figure 2.3).

Segments for Segment Reporting	
Segment	Description
5000	Video Games
5100	Board Games
5200	Card Games
6000	Plush Animals
7000	Toys

Figure 2.3: Definition of segments

The segmentation scenario in the new GL is designed to meet the needs of segment reporting under either IFRS or US-GAAP, however, even if you do not have to file segment-level reports, you may still find some internal use for the segment field in your SAP environment.

Once you have entered the segment in the profit center and saved the master record, you cannot change the value of the `segment` field. It will appear with a grey background and is not directly editable (see Figure 2.4.)

Basic Data		
User Responsible		
Person Respons.	Sally Goround	
Department		
Profit Ctr Group	5000	Smarter Sisters
Segment	5000	

Figure 2.4: Segment field in profit center master

If there have been no postings made to the profit center, you can still change the segment value as long as you have change access in SE16 or SE16N. Use one of the two preceding transactions to access the table called V_FAGL_SEGM_PRCT (see Figure 2.5 and Figure 2.6) and in change mode, set the check box to allow the segment to be changed in the profit center.

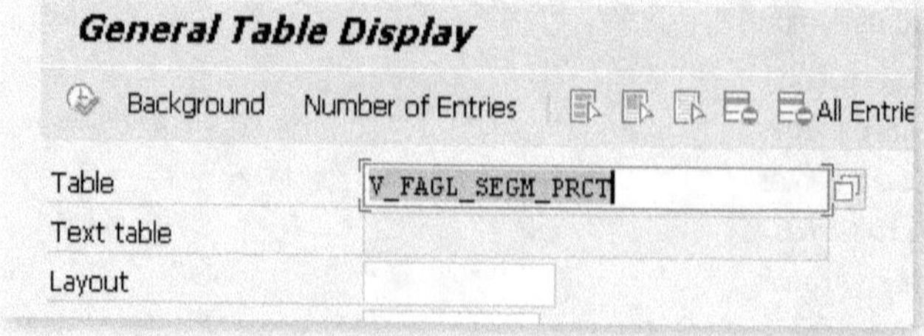

Master data in PCA

```
General Table Display
   Background   Number of Entries   [icons] All Entries
Table            V_FAGL_SEGM_PRCT
Text table
Layout
```

Figure 2.5: Table V_FAGL_SEGM_PRCT

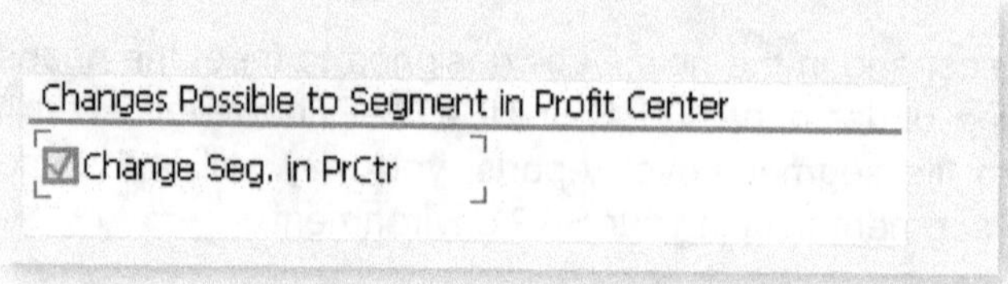

```
Changes Possible to Segment in Profit Center
  ☑ Change Seg. in PrCtr
```

Figure 2.6: Check box to enable change of segment in profit center

The `segment` field is now open for changes in the profit center master (Figure 2.7).

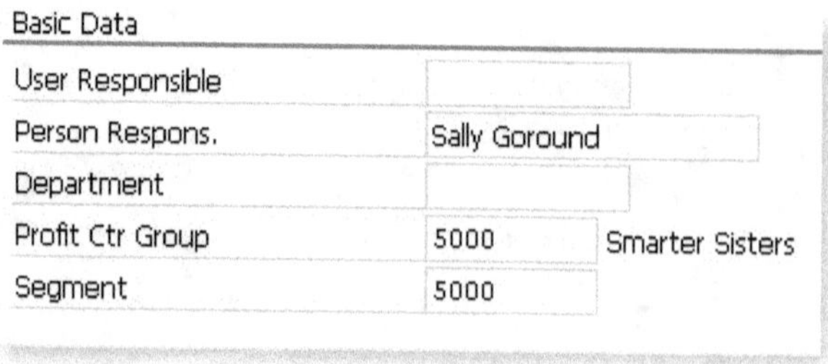

Basic Data		
User Responsible		
Person Respons.	Sally Goround	
Department		
Profit Ctr Group	5000	Smarter Sisters
Segment	5000	

Figure 2.7: Segment field is now editable

Additional control information is found on the INDICATORS tab (see Figure 2.8) and on the COMPANY CODES tab (see Figure 2.9). The HISTORY tab is useful since it shows who created the profit center and when and also provides links to the *change documents*.

On the INDICATORS tab, you can lock the profit center to prevent postings. If the locked profit center is assigned to another object and you try to make a posting using the linked object, you receive an error message and the transaction is not posted.

On the COMPANY CODES tab, you can determine which company codes are assigned to your profit center. By default, if you create the profit center manually, your profit center is linked to all company codes. If you want to restrict this, you need to go into the COMPANY CODES tab and deselect the assignment. The profit center must be assigned to at least one company code.

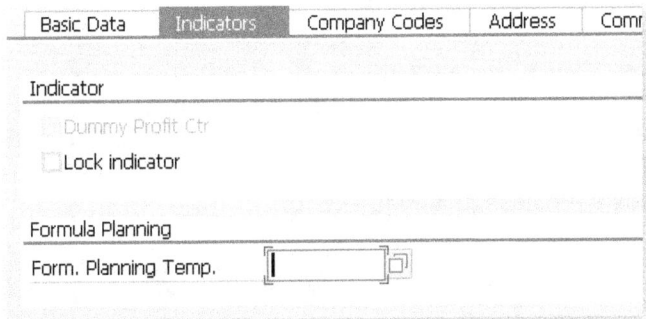

Figure 2.8: Profit center indicators tab

Basic Data	Indicators	Company Codes	Address	Communication
Company Code Assignment for Profit Center				
CoCd	Company Name		Assigned	
5000	Smarter Sisters US		☑	
5100	Smarter Sisters Canada		✓	
5200	Smarter Sisters Europe		✓	
5300	Smarter Sisters Asia		✓	

Figure 2.9: Profit center company code tab

The two other tabs, ADDRESS and COMMUNICATION, allow you to enter the address, tax jurisdiction, language, telephone, fax, etc. for the profit center. If you have a requirement to store this information at the profit center level, then the fields are available, but not mandatory.

Once you have entered your data, you can save your profit center. Unlike other master data in SAP, it is not sufficient to press the 💾 button. If you just press save, you receive a message (see Figure 2.10). You can proceed, but the profit center will be saved in inactive status and will not be able to receive postings.

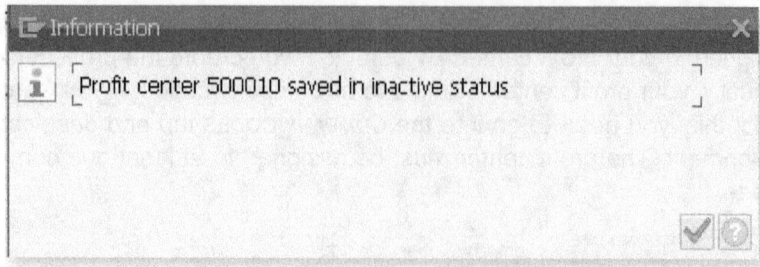

Figure 2.10: Message when saving the profit center

If you want to use the profit center right away, you should click the ACTIVATE button. This will create and save the profit center in active status and you will not see the message in Figure 2.10.

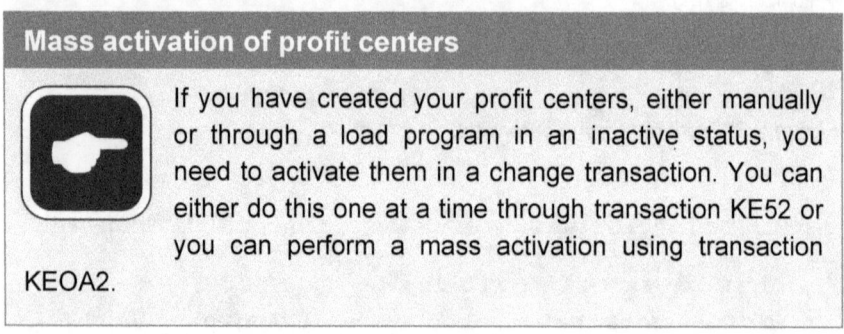

Mass activation of profit centers

If you have created your profit centers, either manually or through a load program in an inactive status, you need to activate them in a change transaction. You can either do this one at a time through transaction KE52 or you can perform a mass activation using transaction KEOA2.

Additionally, when you make changes to the profit center in KE52 you also need to activate the changes.

2.2 The dummy profit center

The definition of the dummy profit center is only required if classic PCA is activated. In classic PCA, the dummy profit center may be posted to when you have neglected to assign a profit center to an object that should have a profit center assignment. This is to make sure that you are still able to reconcile between PCA and financial accounting. In the new GL, this is not the case since the profit center is part of the financial accounting posting and is stored in the FI ledgers rather than in a separate ledger, therefore reconciliation is not needed.

In classic PCA, analysis of the posting to the dummy profit center should be done on a periodic basis to find any missing assignments. The postings in the dummy profit center should also be allocated or reposted to the correct profit centers on a periodic basis.

Only one dummy profit center is required per controlling area and it is created initially using transaction KE59. After that, the dummy profit center can be changed or displayed using the standard transactions KE52 or KE53. The creation of the dummy profit center is almost identical to creating a regular profit center. The only differences are:

- The dummy profit center will automatically be set with a maximum validity period.
- You cannot create a dummy profit center by copying an existing profit center.
- The check box on the profit center INDICATORS tab for dummy profit ctr will be set automatically (see Figure 2.11).

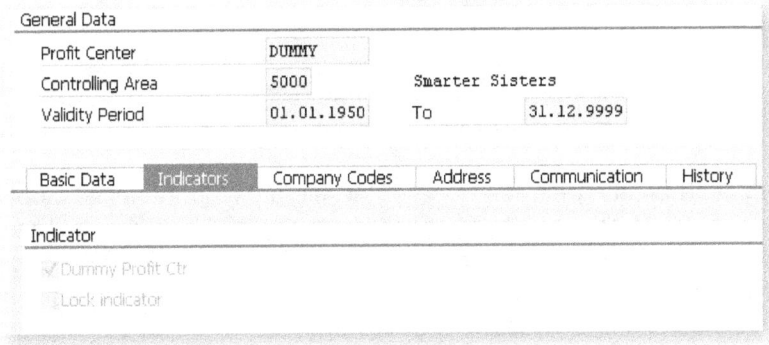

Figure 2.11: Dummy profit center indicator

2.3 Profit center standard hierarchy

It is necessary to define a standard hierarchy for profit centers before you create the profit center master data. This is a hierarchy or tree structure that is assigned to the controlling area. The hierarchy can take any form that you require to represent the structure of your organization. The hierarchy can be built up by creating multiple levels, known as nodes or groups. All of your profit centers must be assigned somewhere within the standard hierarchy.

The standard hierarchy is a particular type of profit center group that requires all the profit centers within the controlling area to be assigned to it. The overall hierarchy, and the groups within it, can be used functionally in SAP for planning, allocations, and reporting. If alternative groupings of profit centers are required for these functions, it is possible to create additional groups which are not linked to the standard hierarchy. This is shown in the next section on profit center groups.

Standard Hierarchy	Name	Activation sta...	Person Respo...
5000	Smarter Sisters		
· DUMMY	DUMMY PC	☐	dummy
5001	Games		
· 50001	US Region		
· 51001	Canada Region		
· 52001	Europe Region		
· 53001	Asia Region		
> 6000	Plush Toys		
> 7000	Toys		

Figure 2.12: Standard hierarchy framework

I recommend creating the top node of the hierarchy in the initial create transaction KCH1 and then building the hierarchy in the change transaction KCH5N. The KCH5N transaction, shown in Figure 2.12, is much easier to use than KCH1 and provides the ability to drag and drop objects into place within the hierarchy structure.

Within KCH5N, you use the CREATE button to create profit center groups (nodes) or profit centers themselves (see Figure 2.13.). The object is created relative to where you have your cursor positioned in the hierarchy. When you create a profit center in this way you will not have to enter the profit center group on the screen, as it will assume the value based on where your cursor is positioned in the hierarchy.

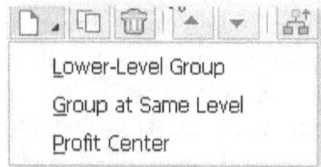

Figure 2.13 Create options within KCH5N

If you create your profit centers at the top node of the hierarchy, as shown in Figure 2.14, you can simply use the mouse to drag and drop the profit center(s) or profit center group(s) into the correct position(s).

Standard Hierarchy	Name	Activation sta...	Person Respo...
5000	Smarter Sisters		
500010	Video Games - US	☐	Sally Goround
500020	Board Games - US	☐	Peter Piper
500030	Card Games - US	☐	Sam Spade
510010	Video Games - CAN	☐	Bruce Berry
510020	Board Games- CAN	☐	Thelma Augustus
510030	Card Games - CAN	☐	Tyler Diamond
520010	Video Games- EUR	☐	Hans Brinker
520020	Board Games- EUR	☐	Martha Midear
520030	Card Games - EUR	☐	Rosa Club
530010	Video Games - ASIA	☐	Sam Lync
530020	Board Games- ASIA	☐	Sherry Baby
530030	Card Games - ASIA	☐	Brigitte Hearts
DUMMY	DUMMY PC	☐	dummy
5001	Games		
50001	US Region		
51001	Canada Region		
52001	Europe Region		
53001	Asia Region		

Figure 2.14: Standard hierarchy with profit centers at top level

Once you drag the profit center(s) to the correct node(s), you can organize them within the node(s) by using the MOVE ▲ ▼ buttons. The hierarchy should now have the profit center(s) assigned to the correct node(s) (see Figure 2.15).

Standard Hierarchy	Name	Activation sta...	Person Respo...
5000	Smarter Sisters		
DUMMY	DUMMY PC	☐	dummy
5001	Games		
50001	US Region		
500010	Video Games - US	☐	Sally Goround
500020	Board Games - US	☐	Peter Piper
500030	Card Games - US	☐	Sam Spade
51001	Canada Region		
510010	Video Games - CAN	☐	Bruce Berry
510020	Board Games- CAN	☐	Thelma Augustus
510030	Card Games - CAN	☐	Tyler Diamond
52001	Europe Region		
520010	Video Games- EUR	☐	Hans Brinker
520020	Board Games- EUR	☐	Martha Midear
520030	Card Games - EUR	☐	Rosa Club
53001	Asia Region		
530010	Video Games - ASIA	☐	Sam Lync
530020	Board Games- ASIA	☐	Sherry Baby
530030	Card Games - ASIA	☐	Brigitte Hearts

Figure 2.15: Standard hierarchy with profit center assigned to nodes

2.4 Profit center group

Groups of master data are commonly used within SAP software to aid with functionality in the areas of planning, allocations, and reporting. Within profit center accounting, you are most likely going to group profit centers to provide alternative reporting views or when using GL allocations. These groups, sometimes referred to as *alternative hierarchies*, share many of the characteristics of the standard hierarchy but do not have to contain all the profit centers in the controlling area. The groups are created in transaction KCH1 and can contain any combination of profit centers organized in any manner (see Figure 2.16). In this example, you want to group profit centers to see a product view of results rather than the more geographical view shown in the standard hierarchy.

The groups can be edited in transaction KCH2. In both KCH1 and KCH2 the same TOOLBAR is available. It has similar functions to the CREATE OPTIONS screen in the standard hierarchy. Other than the general design of the screen, there are two apparent differences between KCH5N and KCH2. First, the simple drag and drop functionality is not available in KCH2, and second, there is a WHERE USED button visible in KCH2. The where used functionality is still available in KCH5N, but you access it from the menu EXTRAS • USE OF GROUP.

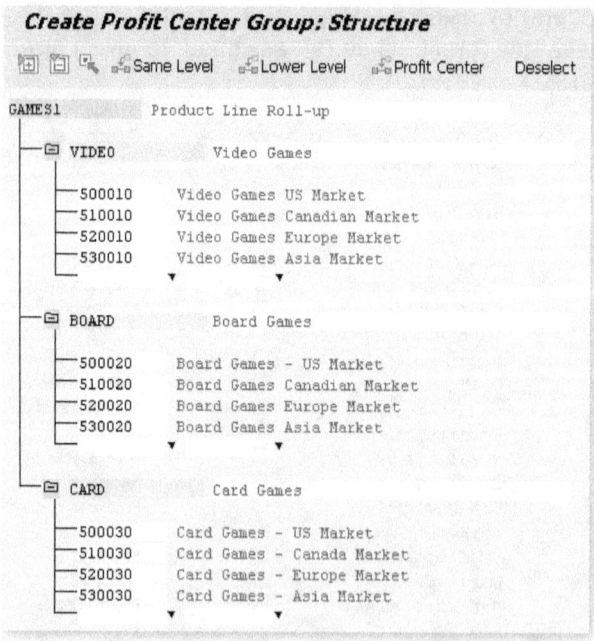

Figure 2.16: Profit center group alternative structure

The moving or deleting of objects in KCH2 is a little less obvious than in KCH5N where you have drag and drop functionality and a TRASH CAN to delete unwanted groups. In KCH2, you need to use the SELECT button to mark an item and then open the menu bar to see new options in the TOOLBAR.

As an example, in Figure 2.17, you see DUMMY PROFIT CENTER is added into the CARD group. You need to remove it.

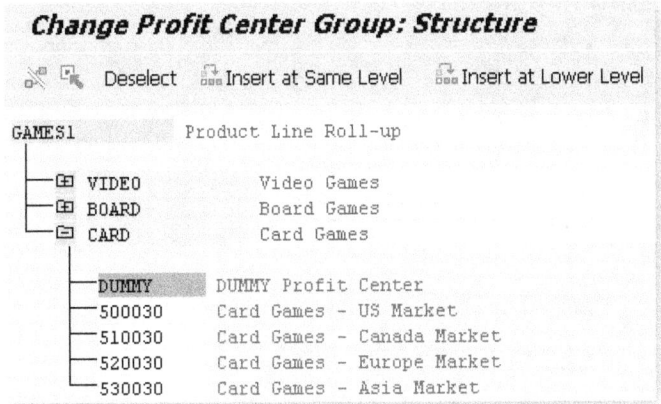

Figure 2.17: Remove unwanted item from the group

I have clicked on the item and pressed the SELECT button. Now from the new TOOLBAR I can select the action that I want. In this case, I want to remove the DUMMY PROFIT CENTER from the group so I click the REMOVE button. I could also use the INSERT option to move items to different places within the group structure.

The final function worth discussing for groups is the WHERE USED button. As mentioned, groups are used to support a variety of functions in SAP. They may be referenced somewhere in the system configuration or may be used in an allocation or within a report painter report. It is always useful to find out where a group is being used before making changes to it. To support this, SAP provides the where used function. Clicking on the button will allow you to select where you want to search for the use of the group (see Figure 2.18) and will return a report showing where the group is used based on what you selected. Figure 2.19 shows the group, VIDEO, in two places. It is contained in the group GAMES and it is used in allocation TEST1 in segment INSURANCE.

35

MASTER DATA IN PCA

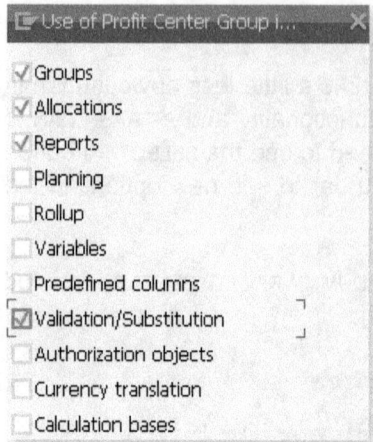

Figure 2.18: Selection for use of profit center groups

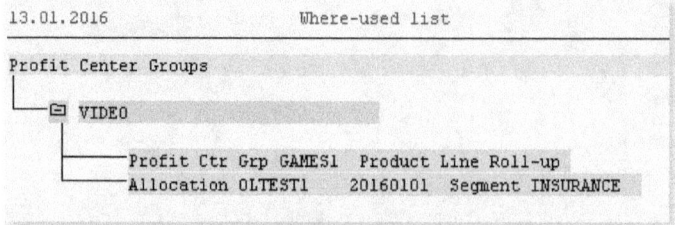

Figure 2.19: Where used report for profit center groups

Moving profit center groups to another SAP system

In an SAP implementation project, there are generally multiple systems involved. There will be at least a development system, a quality or test system, and a production system. Within the development and test systems there may also be multiple clients such as a configuration client, a test client, and a sandbox client. It can be considerable effort to build your groups manually within each of these systems and clients. To assist, SAP has provided an export/import option for groups available under the EXTRAS menu. The group can be exported as a text file to either the SAP file system or to your computer (select the presentation server option) and then imported into another SAP system or client.

The basic create, move, and remove functions shown in the profit center group are standard across all group transactions within the controlling module. The groups for other controlling objects such as *cost centers*, *cost elements*, *internal orders*, *activity types*, and *statistical key figures* can be manipulated in a similar manner to profit center groups.

> ### Segments or groups
>
>  With the new GL, you have the opportunity to assign profit centers to segments. This does not mean that you will not need profit center groups. The segment is primarily for external reporting and does not exist in a hierarchical structure. On the other hand, profit center groups can be created and arranged as needed and can be arranged hierarchically. Another consideration is that the profit center can only be assigned to one segment, whereas multiple groups can be created and each can contain the same profit center.

2.5   Revenue/cost elements and accounts

The accounts used in profit center accounting are based on the *chart of accounts* assigned to the controlling area that you are working in. In classic PCA, these accounts can be classified in the following three ways:

- ▶ Accounts where transactions flow from financial accounting into controlling—there are either revenue elements or primary cost elements in controlling
- ▶ Accounts used for moving costs around in controlling only—these are known as secondary cost elements
- ▶ Accounts in financial accounting where transactions do not flow to controlling—these are normally balance sheet accounts or P&L accounts not assigned to a cost element

In profit center accounting within the new GL, things are slightly different. Since the profit center is contained within the GL, you can potentially have all the accounts within the chart of accounts posting to a profit center. The main difference is that the secondary cost element will no longer post directly to the profit center. If an allocation posting between objects in controlling goes across profit centers, then the posting in financial accounting to the profit center will occur in the GL account defined in the configuration for the account determination for real-time integration between FI and CO. Depending on your system configuration, the real-time FI-CO reconciliation may occur in one account or may be driven by rules and use a number of different accounts.

2.6 Account groups

Within profit center accounting, you can create hierarchical structures of accounts. Within classic PCA, these account groups can be used in planning, allocations, and reporting functions in a similar way to profit center or other master data groups with SAP Controlling. The use of account groups in PCA is entirely optional and a standard hierarchy of accounts is not required.

The account group is created in transaction KDH1 (see Figure 2.20) and the creation and maintenance of the group is similar to KSH1.

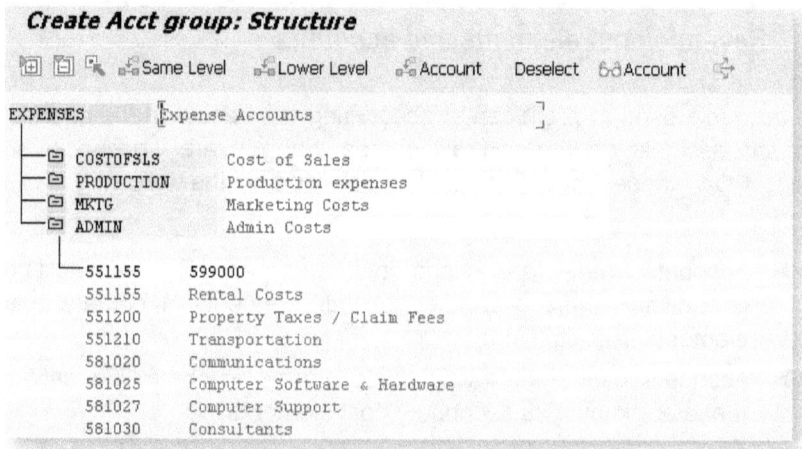

Figure 2.20: Account group structure

> **Copy account groups**
>
>  SAP provides two transactions to allow you to create account groups based on existing data in your system. Transaction KE61 allows you to select a cost element group that has previously been defined in controlling and copy it as an account group in PCA. Transaction KE5B allows you to copy a financial statement version from financial accounting. This copy will bring in all the levels of the financial statement version as account groups in a hierarchy structure.

Account groups seem to have less usefulness in the new GL world. They are not used in planning in the new GL and are not available as a selection option in the GL reports in the information system. It is still possible to select the account group within GL distribution and assessment as a value in the sender section by entering the account group in the SET field. *Sets* are objects that SAP uses to group data and maintain hierarchies. A set, or multiple sets, will be created behind the scenes when you create groups in SAP Controlling.

2.7 Statistical key figures

Statistical key figures (SKFs) can be created as master data in SAP Controlling and used to define some measurable value that you wish to attribute to a controlling object such as a cost center, profit center, or internal order. The figure should represent some statistic or numerical value above and beyond the currency amount posting that you wish to track for that cost object. Some examples of statistical key figures include: headcount, number of computers, kilowatt hours of electricity consumed, and number of purchase orders issued. The SKF will display on reports for the associated object and is often used as a factor to drive allocations.

Statistical key figure functionality is also available in the new GL and SKFs can be posted against a variety of objects in the GL, including cost center, profit center, and segment. In the new GL, it is important to realize that planned and actual SKF postings from controlling objects will pass into the new GL based on real-time integration between FI and CO. This means that you do not need to repeat SKF postings on the FI side if they are posted to the same SKF and cost object in CO.

Statistical key figures may be used as an allocation base or *tracing factor* within allocations in both CO and FI. They will also be reported on a number of standard SAP reports and could be used as the basis of analytical calculations, such as cost per employee.

Regardless of where you are using the SKF, the master data is only created in one place with transaction KK01. The statistical key figure is created within the controlling area (see Figure 2.21) and is available for posting to objects assigned to that controlling area.

Create Statistical Key Figure: Initial Screen

Master Data

Controlling Area	5000
Stat. key figure	HCNT

Copy from

Stat. key figure	
Controlling Area	

Figure 2.21: Create SKF initial screen

The SKF is a simple piece of master data with only a few fields to complete (see Figure 2.22). You must give an alphanumeric identifier to the SKF, then to create it, you must give it a name, assign a unit of measure based on the units available in your SAP system, and decide on whether the SKF will be treated as a fixed value SKF or a total values SKF.

The purpose or nature of the statistic that you are tracking should determine the fixed or total setting. The general definition is:

- The fixed value gets carried over from the original posting to all subsequent periods in the same fiscal year. You only need to make a new posting if the value changes. This should be used for statistics that remain relatively constant over time, such as headcount.
- The total values amount does not transfer to the following period. Therefore, it needs to be entered every period. This is more useful for things like number of units produced in a period.

Create Statistical Key Figure: Master Data

Link to LIS		
Stat. key figure	HCNT	
Controlling area	5000	Smarter Sisters

Basic data		
Name	Employee Headcount	
Stat. key fig. UnM.	PRS	Number of Persons
Key fig. cat.	● Fxd val.	
	○ Tot. values	

Figure 2.22: Create SKF master data fields

The LINK TO LIS button allows you to link a statistical key figure to a key figure in the logistics information structure (LIS). Click on the LINK button and then search by INFO STRUCTURE or by INFO SET. Then look in the selected application for the key figure to link to your SKF. Once you make the link, you'll see it reflected in your SKF (see Figure 2.23). Once you have linked your SKFs, you can transfer the LIS values periodically to the SKFs in controlling.

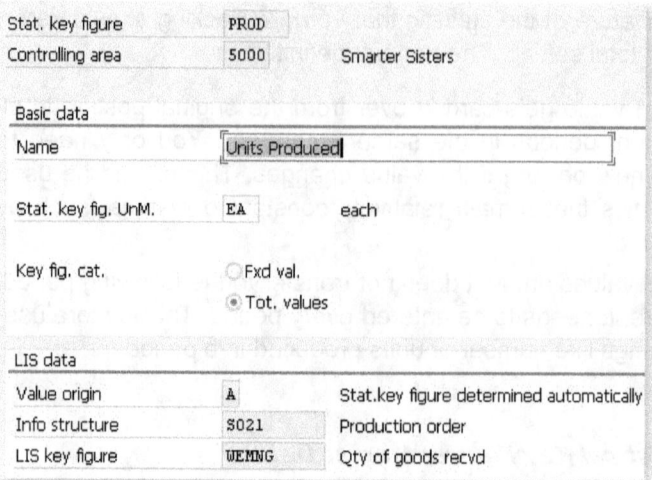

Figure 2.23: Link SKF to LIS

In the new GL, SKF values will flow from controlling to financial accounting based on the real-time integration between FI and CO. Similar functionality can be activated in classic PCA where you can choose whether SKFs will have postings transferred from cost objects to profit centers based on assigning the SKF in the configuration. Use transaction 3KEG to choose statistical key figures (see Figure 2.24).

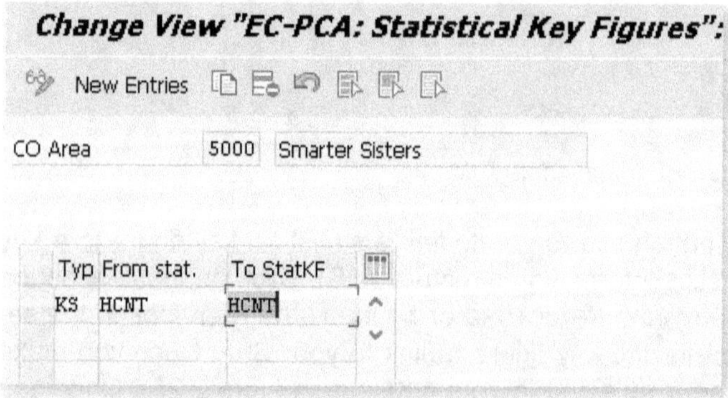

Figure 2.24: Transfer SKF from controlling to PCA

2.8 Profit center assignment

In the ideal situation, you should not have to manually enter the profit center into any transaction in SAP. In both classic PCA and the new GL, the profit center should be automatically derived in the posting. This automatic derivation is generally a result of the assignment of profit centers to other pieces of master data in SAP. Profit center derivation can also be achieved through the use of substitution rules and in the new GL there is an option to assign a default profit center to an account in the configuration.

If you are using profit center accounting, then you should ensure that the following objects are assigned to a profit center—assuming that you are using the object in your environment:

- Cost centers
- Internal orders
- Work breakdown structures in project systems
- Networks in project systems
- Business processes in activity-based costing
- Material masters
- Production and/or process orders
- Product cost collectors in repetitive manufacturing
- Sales order items
- Plant maintenance orders
- Fixed assets

The assignment of profit centers to the objects listed above should ensure that you do not have to manually enter profit centers into your transactions. Assignment of other controlling objects to a profit center is done by manually filling in the PROFIT CENTER field on the other master data object(s). This will be true for the first five items in the preceding list.

For cost centers, this is on the BASIC DATA tab on the cost center master (see Figure 2.25). If you create your cost center master through the cost center standard hierarchy, then you see the PROFIT CENTER field on the ORGANIZATION tab.

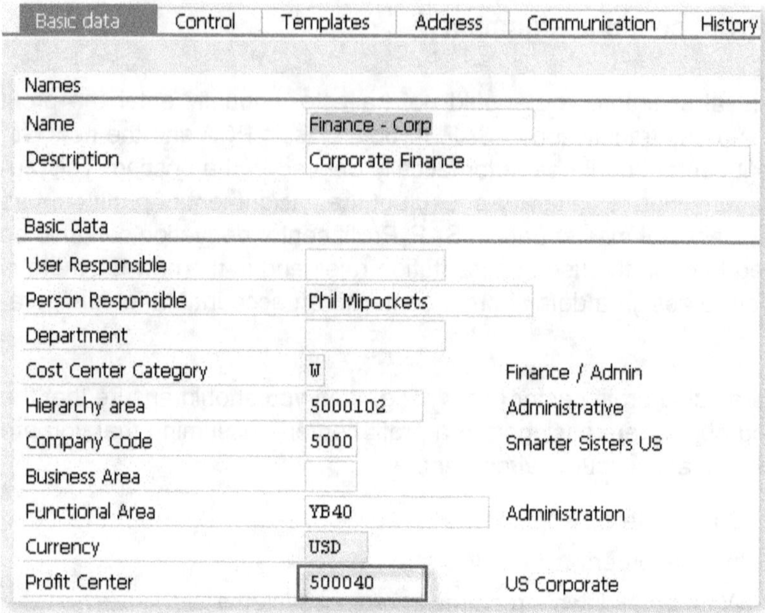

Master data in PCA

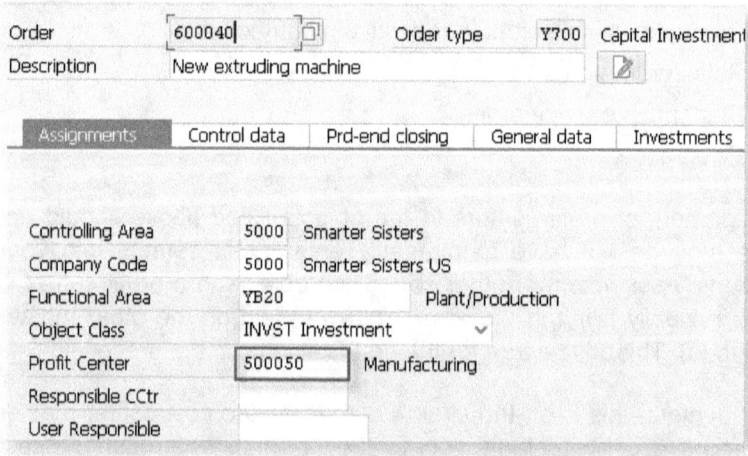

Figure 2.25: Assign a profit center to a cost center

The assignment is similar for the internal order. The profit center is assigned on the ASSIGNMENTS tab (see Figure 2.26).

Figure 2.26: Assign a profit center to an internal order

In project systems, you have four possible places to assign the profit center. You can assign the profit center to the *project profile* in configuration transaction OPSA on the organization tab (see Figure 2.27). The profit center assigned here will come into any project created with this profile as a default value on the BASIC DATA tab (see Figure 2.28.). This is also the second place that you can assign a profit center in project systems. If no profit center is set in the project profile, this will appear blank and you can assign your default profit center here when you create the project. You can also change the default that is brought in from the project profile.

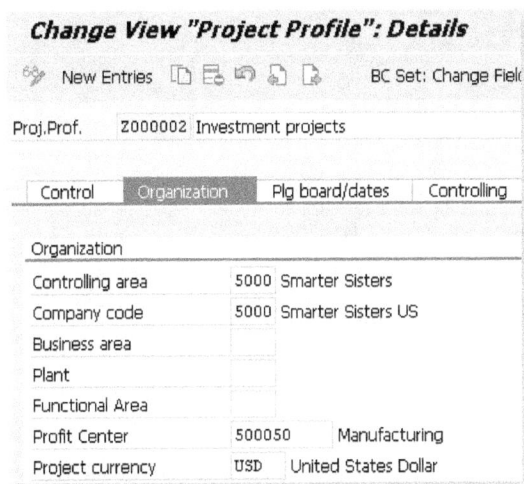

Figure 2.27: Profit center on the project profile

Organization	
CO area	5000
Company code	5000
Business area	
Plant	
Location	
Functional Area	
Profit Center	500050
Proj.currency	USD

Figure 2.28: Profit center with an organization setting on a project

45

The profit center at the project level is a default value that gets passed to any WBS elements or networks that are created below it. Depending on how you are using project systems, the WBS element, the network, and/or the network activity may serve as a cost object. The profit center assignment at the lower levels will default from the project and can also be maintained manually on the object. On the WBS element, the network and the activity for the profit center can be maintained on the ASSIGNMENT tab. Since the assignment is similar for all the objects, I only show the WBS element in Figure 2.29.

Basic Data	Dates	Assignments		Control
Organization				
CO area	5000			Subproject
Company code	5000			Plant
Bus.area				Location
Functional Area	YB20			Factory cale
Profit Center	500050			Equipment
Object Class	INVST Investment			Functional I
Currency	USD			Change Nur

Figure 2.29: Assign a profit center to a WBS element

In SAP, a *business process* is the controlling master data object used in *activity-based costing*. The simplest definition is that the business process is a cost object used for receiving costs from cost objects, such as cost centers, and re-distributing the costs to other objects, such as production orders, other cost centers, internal orders, or profitability segments based on activity-related rules. The business process exists under the controlling area but is independent of any one cost center. In fact, the business process can involve activities from a number of different cost centers. If PCA is active, profit centers should be assigned to each controlling object, so you need to assign a profit center to the business process. This is assigned in the BASIC DATA tab of the business process master record (see Figure 2.30).

The cost object items shown should have a profit center manually assigned to them when they are created and this profit center will then be derived into any transaction using that cost object.

The material master in SAP can be a complex piece of master data. The layout of the data and the tabs that are available are controlled by the material type that you select when you create the material. For example, the raw material, material type ROH, may not require sales tabs while finished good type FERT will. In addition, the same material master can be extended for various organization objects such as sales organization or plant. This creates organization-specific views of the data. In this way, the same material master record can be used for a variety of plants or sales organizations, but can contain different data values in the organization-specific views.

Business Process	5000-100	Product Design	
Controlling Area	5000	Smarter Sisters	
Valid From	01.01.2010	to	31.12.9999

Basic Data	Organization	Attributes	Allocation	Templates

Descriptions	
Name	Product Design
Description	Product Design

Basic Data		
Person Responsible		
Person Responsible		
Hierarchy Area	P5000_HIER	Standard Hierarchy for 5000
Company Code	5000	Smarter Sisters US
Business Area		
Object Currency	USD	US Dollar
Profit Center	500050	Manufacturing

Figure 2.30: Profit center assigned to a business process

This is important from a profit center assignment perspective for the following two reasons. First, a profit center is considered plant specific, so it will be possible to have multiple profit centers assigned to the same material number, but only one per plant. Second, because of the tabular nature of the material master and the fact that certain tabs may not be selected for certain material types, the profit center field actually appears on three different tabs in the material master. The fact that it appears three times does not mean you can have three different values. Once you enter the profit center value in one of the three places, it will also populate any of the other fields on the tabs listed below.

- ▶ Plant data storage 2 (Figure 2.31)
- ▶ Costing data 1 (Figure 2.32)
- ▶ Sales general/plant (Figure 2.33)

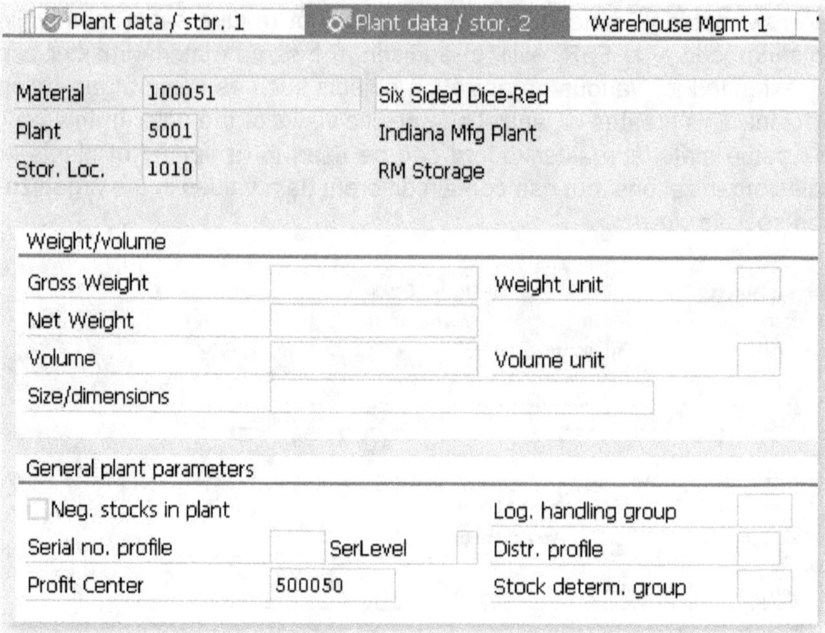

MASTER DATA IN PCA

| Plant data / stor. 1 | Plant data / stor. 2 | Warehouse Mgmt 1 |

Material	100051	Six Sided Dice-Red
Plant	5001	Indiana Mfg Plant
Stor. Loc.	1010	RM Storage

Weight/volume

Gross Weight		Weight unit	
Net Weight			
Volume		Volume unit	
Size/dimensions			

General plant parameters

☐ Neg. stocks in plant		Log. handling group	
Serial no. profile		SerLevel	Distr. profile	
Profit Center	500050	Stock determ. group	

Figure 2.31: Material master plant data/stor 2

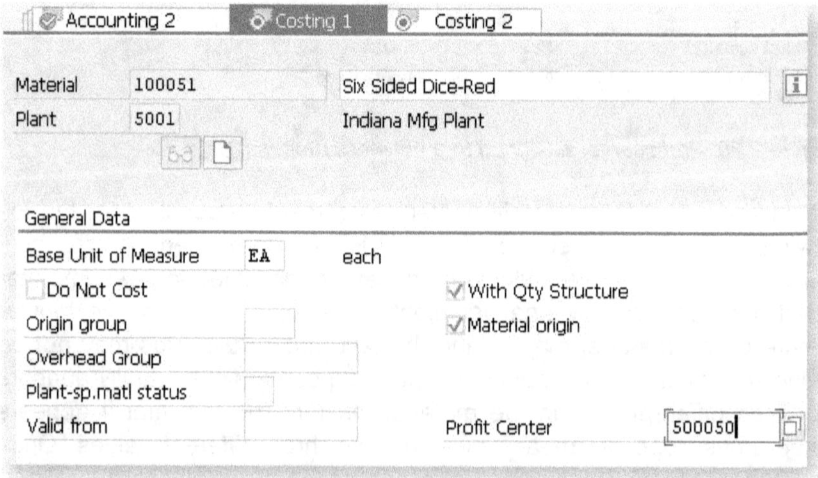

| Accounting 2 | Costing 1 | Costing 2 |

Material	100051	Six Sided Dice-Red
Plant	5001	Indiana Mfg Plant

General Data

Base Unit of Measure	EA	each	
☐ Do Not Cost		☑ With Qty Structure	
Origin group		☑ Material origin	
Overhead Group			
Plant-sp.matl status			
Valid from		Profit Center	500050

Figure 2.32: Material master costing 1

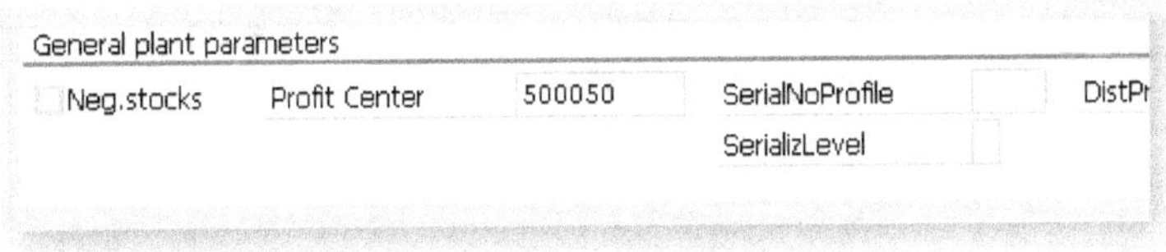

General plant parameters					
Neg.stocks	Profit Center	500050	SerialNoProfile		DistPr
			SerializLevel		

Figure 2.33: Material master sales general/plant view

The profit center from the material master is passed into relevant objects that are created using that material, such as production orders, process orders, and product cost collectors. The profit center on the material is also used as the default profit center on the sales order line containing that material.

Manufacturing in SAP can take many forms and can use a variety of orders as cost objects. In a make-to-stock environment, it is possible to use production orders, process orders, or repetitive manufacturing using the product cost collector. On the other hand, you can have a make-to-order or engineer-to-order scenario where you may use the sales order items either alone or in combination with production orders or projects as the cost object. In all of these cases the cost object should have a profit center assigned. In most cases, this will come from the material being produced.

In the case of make-to-stock production, the profit center will be on the header of either the production or process order on the ASSIGNMENTS tab (Figure 2.34).

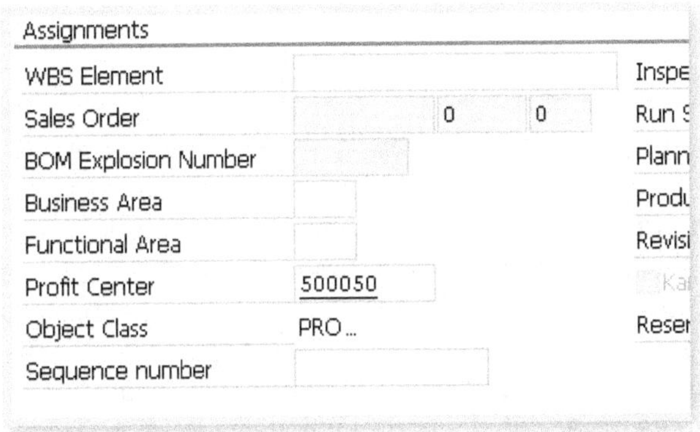

Assignments				
WBS Element				Inspe
Sales Order		0	0	Run S
BOM Explosion Number				Plann
Business Area				Produ
Functional Area				Revisi
Profit Center	500050			Ka
Object Class	PRO...			Reser
Sequence number				

Figure 2.34: Production order header—assignments

For repetitive manufacturing, the profit center will be on the data view of the product cost collector (see Figure 2.35).

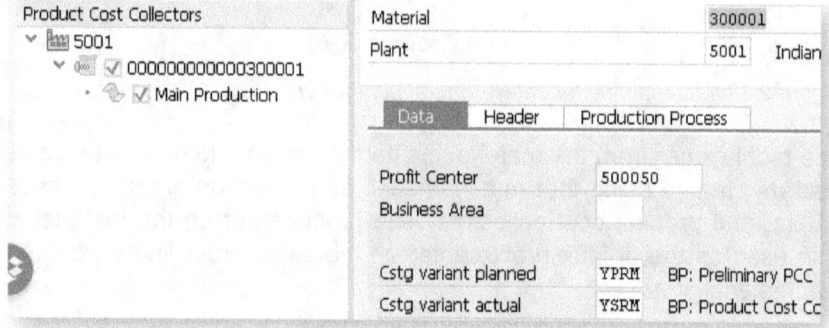

Figure 2.35: Product cost collector

For a normal sales order, the profit center will appear on the ACCOUNT ASSIGNMENT tab on the sales order line. This will default based on the material contained on that line (see Figure 2.36).

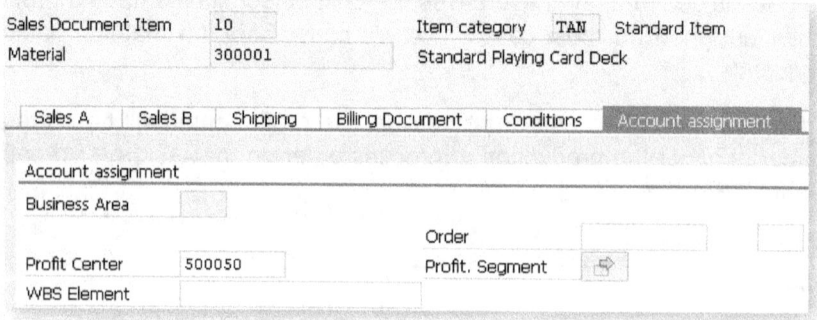

Figure 2.36: Profit center assigned to sales order item

There are situations where you may not wish to have the material master profit center used on the sales order. For example, you might have a profit center that represents the production plant on the material, but you want to have a profit center that represents your geographical or division-based reporting structure on the sales order. For such a requirement, you can make use of the *sales order substitution* functionality in PCA. This is accessed through configuration transaction 0KEM. In this transaction, you can build a substitution based on a number of steps that will allow you to substitute the profit center on the sales order based on certain prerequisite values defined in your substitution (see Figure 2.37).

Master data in PCA

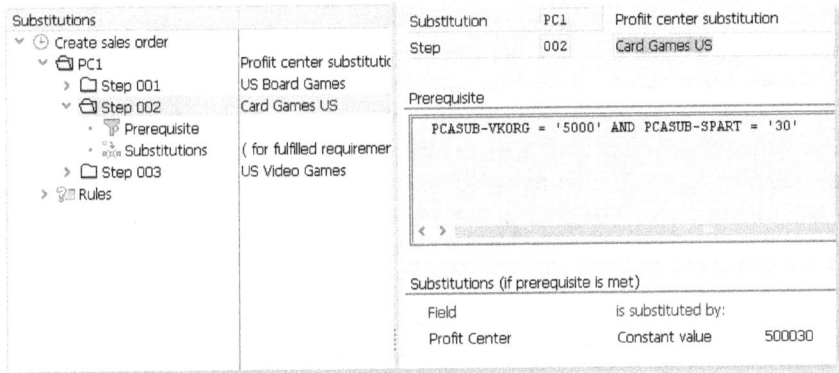

Figure 2.37: Profit center substitution for sales order

Once you have built your profit center substitution, you need to assign it to your controlling area and choose the activation option. This is done in configuration transaction OKEL (see Figure 2.38). There are five activation options available under the active status.

- Blank—The substitution is not called and the profit center will be derived from the material master.
- 1—The substitution is used for all normal sales documents, but only for billing documents in a cross-company scenario.
- 2—The substitution is only done in a cross-company billing document.
- 3—The substitution is used for all normal sales documents and all sales documents in a cross-company scenario.
- 4—The substitution is only done in a cross-company scenario for all sales documents.

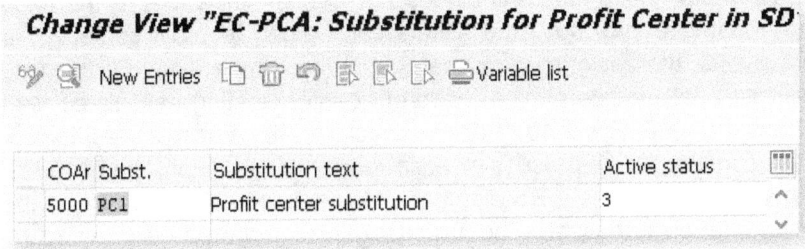

Figure 2.38: Assign and activate substitution

51

Once your substitution is active, the profit center determined by your rule will appear in the sales order line rather than the profit center from the material master.

Plant maintenance orders are objects that allow the scheduling, tracking, and reporting of maintenance activities. In part, they behave as a cost object similar to other cost collecting orders in SAP such as internal or production orders. On the maintenance order, the profit center is assigned on the ADDITIONAL DATA tab (see Figure 2.39). The profit center will automatically populate based on the *responsible cost center* in the maintenance order. This value is in turn derived from the maintenance *work center* which was entered on the HEADER DATA tab of the maintenance order.

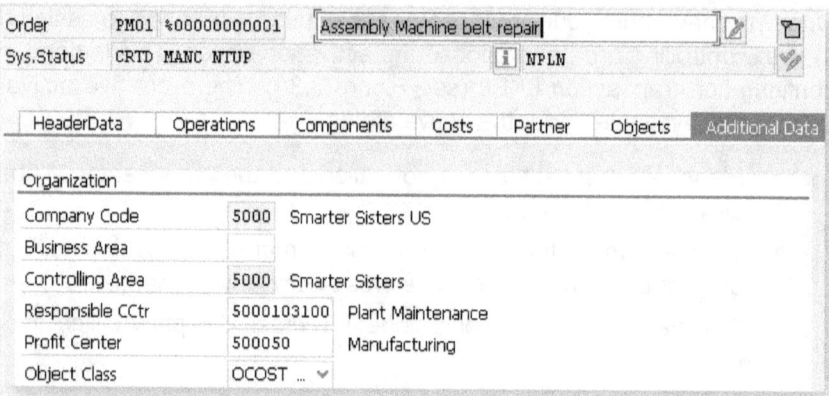

Figure 2.39: Profit center assignment maintenance order

The *fixed asset* in financial accounting is a master data object that can represent a tangible or intangible capital asset belonging to the organization. Normally, the profit center does not appear anywhere in the fixed asset master record, but fixed assets can belong to profit centers. For most assets, the assignment of the cost center to the asset on the TIME DEPENDENT tab will determine the profit center posting associated with that asset (see Figure 2.40). For the special class of assets used to represent construction in process or asset under construction, the associated internal order or the WBS element on the ORIGIN tab will determine the profit center on the asset. If both a cost center and an order or WBS element is assigned to the asset, then the profit center on the order or WBS element will take precedence.

Business function activation

Since the release of SAP ECC version 6.0, SAP has been releasing technical and functional upgrades through enhancement packs. These enhancement packs contain business functions that can be activated in your system if required. Business function FIN_GL_REORG_1 became available in enhancement pack 5. Among other things, this allows activation of segment reporting for asset accounting. This activation allows segment and profit center fields to be available on the TIME DEPENDENT tab of the asset master. Before activating business functions, users should thoroughly read the documentation and fully understand the implications of activating the function. Many business function activations cannot be reversed and some will have a license impact for your SAP system

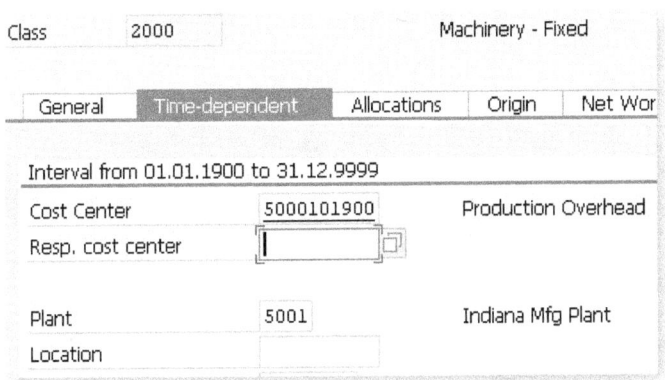

Figure 2.40: Cost center on asset master

Make profit center mandatory

If you are relying on the correct profit center coming into your postings and want to avoid posting to the dummy profit center, then you should make the profit center a required field on as many of the master data objects as you can. For many of these objects, this can be done through the field status settings in your configuration.

53

Once you have maintained your assignments, you can use transaction 1KE4 ASSIGNMENT MONITOR to check on them (see Figure 2.41). This reporting transaction allows you to determine if any objects are not assigned to profit centers and also allows you to report which profit centers are assigned to particular objects or groups of objects. In the case of materials, there is also an option to enter the material mass maintenance transaction, which should be used with care, to make mass changes to fields in the material master. If you are getting incorrect profit center postings or postings to the dummy profit center, the assignment monitor is a useful tool to use to identify missing or incorrect assignments.

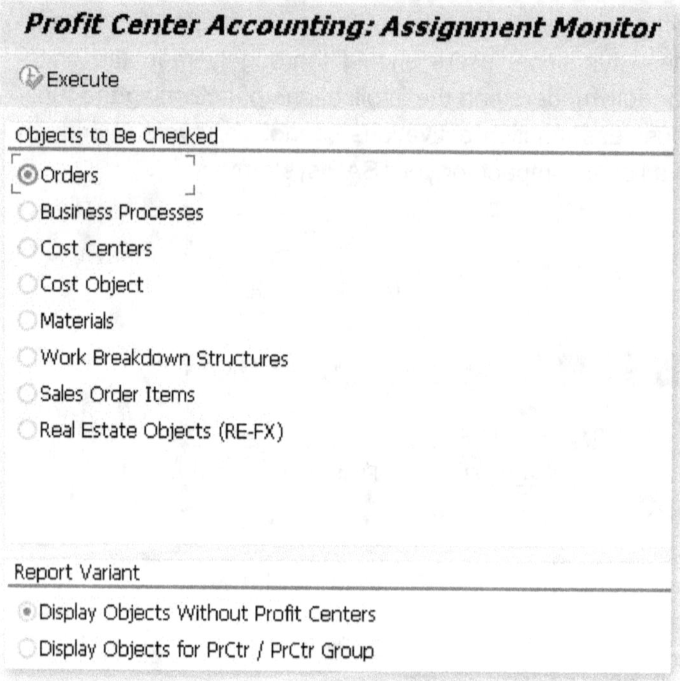

Profit Center Accounting: Assignment Monitor

⊕ Execute

Objects to Be Checked

⦿ Orders
○ Business Processes
○ Cost Centers
○ Cost Object
○ Materials
○ Work Breakdown Structures
○ Sales Order Items
○ Real Estate Objects (RE-FX)

Report Variant

⦿ Display Objects Without Profit Centers
○ Display Objects for PrCtr / PrCtr Group

Figure 2.41: Profit center assignment monitor main screen

> **Profit center reorganization**
>
>  As of enhancement pack 5, SAP has provided a new tool for profit center reorganization which requires the activation of business function FIN_GL_REORG_1. Note that activation of this function may have a license impact. It is applicable to profit center accounting in the new GL only and not classic PCA. The reorganization assists in dividing up, combining, and replacing profit centers. There is an ability to change the profit center assignment on the objects listed previously, at a future key date. The reassignment of objects causes a reassignment of balances in the new GL. For example, if a material is reassigned, its stock inventory balance in the GL will also be reassigned.
>
> The documentation from SAP states that profit center reorganization should be set up as a separate project and be tested rigorously. The documentation also points out that there may be many other prerequisites that need to be met before the reorganization can be started. More details are available in the release notes and prerequisites for the business function and in SAP note 1810605.

2.9 Summary

In this chapter, you have learned about the master data objects that are available within profit center accounting in both the classic and new GL scenarios. You have learned about the concept of groups and hierarchies and how they may be used for planning, allocations, and reporting within SAP. You have also seen in some detail how profit centers are assigned to other objects in SAP so that they can be derived automatically into postings. You will see the effects of this assignment through the next three chapters as you look at planning and actual values flows within profit center accounting.

3 Planning in classic PCA

In this chapter, I explain how planning in classic PCA fits into the overall annual planning cycle for an organization. I demonstrate the integration between the planning functions in other controlling modules such as COPA and overhead cost controlling with classic PCA. Finally, I show you the manual planning tools available in classic PCA.

3.1 How profit center planning fits

Most organizations go through an annual budgeting or planning cycle in order to forecast their revenues and expenses for the upcoming fiscal year. This planning cycle can involve a number of steps in order to get to the overall plan for the enterprise. Depending on the nature of the business, there will likely be a sales plan which will translate into planned revenue and cost of sales, then there may be a production plan which will determine resource requirements and inputs for manufacturing. Finally, there will be an overhead plan incorporating input from overhead cost centers and human resources.

Ideally, you would build your overall plan without having to re-enter the same planning data into different modules within the system. It would make sense that all these planning pieces should ultimately feed into PCA since, in the classic scenario, profit center accounting is the one place where you can get complete P&L statements.

Since planning cycles can vary greatly between organizations, the cycle that is being presented in Figure 3.1 should be considered as a generic example. The unique requirement of each enterprise means that there will have to be individual changes to the process in each company.

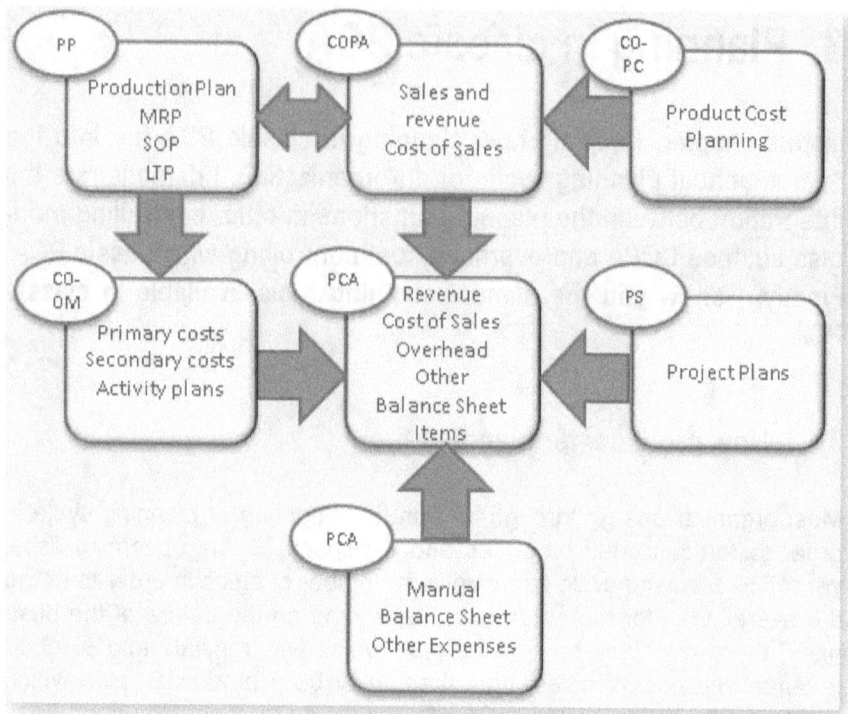

Figure 3.1: Generic planning cycle

Generally, the logical starting point for annual planning is the sales plan. The sales plan is usually defined by the sales department. This may be entered in the planning framework in COPA using transaction KEPM. This is where you define the characteristics that you wish to plan. There are many ways to define planning levels in KEPM. For example, you may want to plan sales quantity by sales organization, product, customer, and plant, or you may just want it by sales organization and product. Within COPA, it is possible to generate planned revenue and cost of sales numbers using valuation. The details of COPA planning are beyond the scope of this book and are just being discussed here because they are part of the integrated planning cycle.

In the overhead management section of controlling, plans can be entered for either cost centers or internal orders that can integrate into your profit center plan. These would be the equivalent of departmental budgets and planning for small overhead projects. Plans entered into project systems at the WBS element level can also integrate with PCA planning. Finally, manual planning can be used to plan additional revenue or expense items or balance sheet items if required.

3.2 Planning version concept in SAP

Throughout controlling, project systems, and also in the new general ledger accounting, the concept of *plan versions* forms the basis of the planning concept. Versions make it possible to store different plans in parallel for the same controlling object. This allows you to maintain and report against different plans based on different conditions, such as a plan based on a favorable sales forecast versus a plan based on a more pessimistic sales forecast. Often, plan versions are used for storing forecasts. A business might start with an original plan and then every quarter update the plan based on history and a new projection, and store the result in a new plan version.

The plan versions are maintained at a general level (see Figure 3.2) for controlling and at a lower level for each controlling area, operating concern, and profit center accounting. Within the controlling area and profit center accounting, the plan version settings are also maintained by fiscal year.

General Version Definition

New Entries

Dialog Structure
- General Version Definition
  - Settings in Operating Concern
  - Settings for Profit Center Account
  - Controlling Area Settings
    - Settings for Each Fiscal Year
    - Delta Version: Bus. Transaction

General Version Overview

Version	Name	Plan	Actual	WIP/RA	Variance
0	Plan/actual version	✓	✓	✓	✓
1	First Quarter Forecast	✓			✓
2	Second Quarter Forecast	✓			✓
3	Third Quarter Forecast	✓			✓

Figure 3.2: Plan versions at a general level

You must have one plan or actual version that can store both plan and actual data, after that you can create as many other plan versions as you require. Additional plan versions must be created at the general level before they can be used in either controlling, COPA, or PCA. At the lower levels, you may use some of the plan versions maintained at the general level.

As mentioned, the versions for profit center accounting and each controlling area have to be maintained by fiscal year (see Figure 3.3). For each planning year, you can maintain the control parameters in the version. You can set the online transfer indicator here (explained in the section on integrated cost planning). It is possible to lock the version by year, which is useful once you have finished your planning and want to prevent any further changes being made. The line-item indicator controls whether line items are created for each change made to plan data, which is useful for being able to track plan changes. Finally, the exchange rate type and value date (not visible on the screen) are used to determine the rate used to translate plan data entered manually.

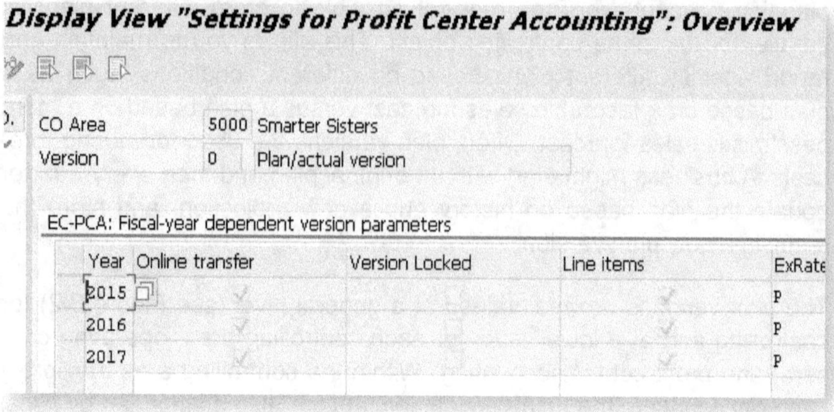
Display View "Settings for Profit Center Accounting": Overview
CO Area
5000
Smarter Sisters
Version
0
Plan/actual version
EC-PCA: Fiscal-year dependent version parameters
Year
Online transfer
Version Locked
Line items
ExRate
2015
P
2016
P
2017
P

Figure 3.3: Plan version for profit center accounting

3.3 Integrated revenue and COGS planning

As mentioned, revenue planning should start in COPA. The sales quantity plan can be entered or loaded into COPA and the *valuation* function in COPA planning transaction KEPM can be used to calculate the revenues and costs based on the entered quantity (see Figure 3.4). These calculated values can then be transferred to PCA.

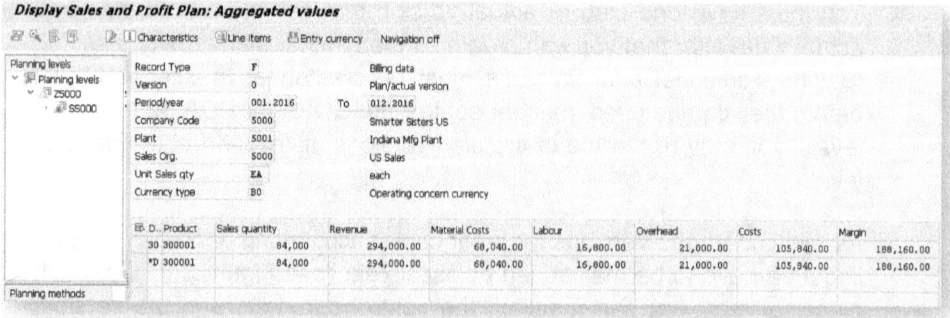
Display Sales and Profit Plan: Aggregated values
Characteristics
Line items
Entry currency
Navigation off
Planning levels
Planning levels
Z5000
SS000
Planning methods
Record Type
F
Billing data
Version
0
Plan/actual version
Period/year
001.2016
To
012.2016
Company Code
5000
Smarter Sisters US
Plant
5001
Indiana Mfg Plant
Sales Org.
5000
US Sales
Unit Sales qty
EA
each
Currency type
B0
Operating concern currency
D.. Product
Sales quantity
Revenue
Material Costs
Labour
Overhead
Costs
Margin
30 300001
84,000
294,000.00
68,040.00
16,800.00
21,000.00
105,840.00
188,160.00
*D 300001
84,000
294,000.00
68,040.00
16,800.00
21,000.00
105,840.00
188,160.00

Figure 3.4: Valuated plan data in COPA

You may recall that there is a major difference between how costing-based COPA handles values versus how they are handled in the other parts of controlling and in the GL. In costing-based COPA, the values are stored in value fields rather than the accounts used in PCA. Before you can transfer your plan from costing-based COPA to PCA, you need to configure a mapping of the value fields to the accounts used in PCA planning in transaction KEDP (see Figure 3.5). Depending on your requirements, you may also have to configure sign switching for the value fields so that they come into PCA as positive or negative.

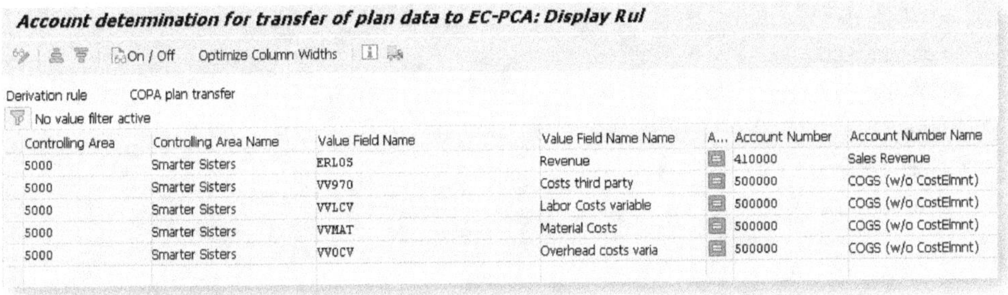

Account determination for transfer of plan data to EC-PCA: Display Rul

Derivation rule   COPA plan transfer
No value filter active

Controlling Area	Controlling Area Name	Value Field Name	Value Field Name Name	A...	Account Number	Account Number Name
5000	Smarter Sisters	ERLOS	Revenue		410000	Sales Revenue
5000	Smarter Sisters	VV970	Costs third party		500000	COGS (w/o CostElmnt)
5000	Smarter Sisters	VVLCV	Labor Costs variable		500000	COGS (w/o CostElmnt)
5000	Smarter Sisters	VVMAT	Material Costs		500000	COGS (w/o CostElmnt)
5000	Smarter Sisters	VVOCV	Overhead costs varia		500000	COGS (w/o CostElmnt)

Figure 3.5: Mapping value fields to accounts

Once the system is configured to map the value fields to the accounts, you can use transaction KE1V to transfer plan data from costing-based COPA. This transaction has several steps within it and it is worth examining each step in detail. The initial screen (shown in Figure 3.6) lets you enter the periods to be transferred along with the version and the record type from COPA. There are also three buttons to select in sequence to complete the transfer process.

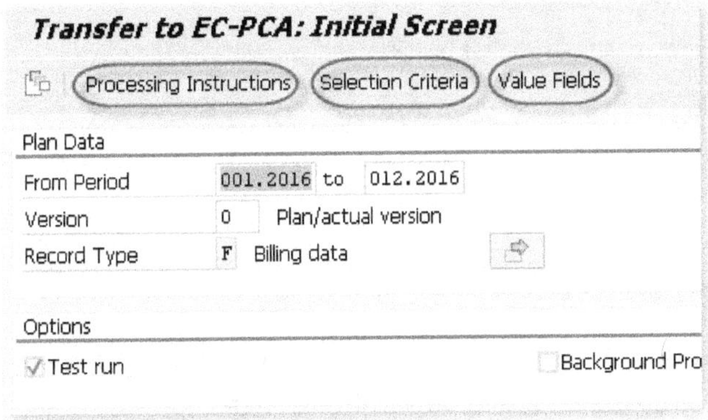

Transfer to EC-PCA: Initial Screen

(Processing Instructions) (Selection Criteria) (Value Fields)

Plan Data
From Period   001.2016 to 012.2016
Version   0   Plan/actual version
Record Type   F   Billing data

Options
☑ Test run   ☐ Background Pro

Figure 3.6: KE1V initial screen

When you select PROCESSING INSTRUCTIONS, you see an additional screen (see Figure 3.7) which allows you to decide whether to directly copy the characteristic as is from COPA or whether to summarize the data based on a characteristic.

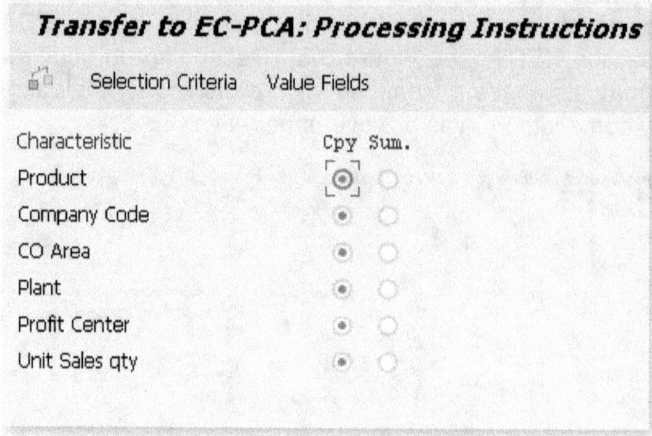

Figure 3.7: KE1V processing instructions

The next step is the SELECTION CRITERIA screen (see Figure 3.8). This allows you to limit the selection of data to be transferred based on characteristic values.

Characteristic	Char. value	Name
Product	*	
Company Code	5000	Smarter Sisters US
CO Area	5000	Smarter Sisters
Plant	5001	Indiana Mfg Plant
Profit Center	*	
Unit Sales qty	*	

Figure 3.8: KE1V selection criteria

Finally, there is the VALUE FIELDS screen (Figure 3.9) where you select which values from your COPA plan you want to transfer to PCA. These should be the same value fields that you mapped to accounts in KEDP.

Planning in classic PCA

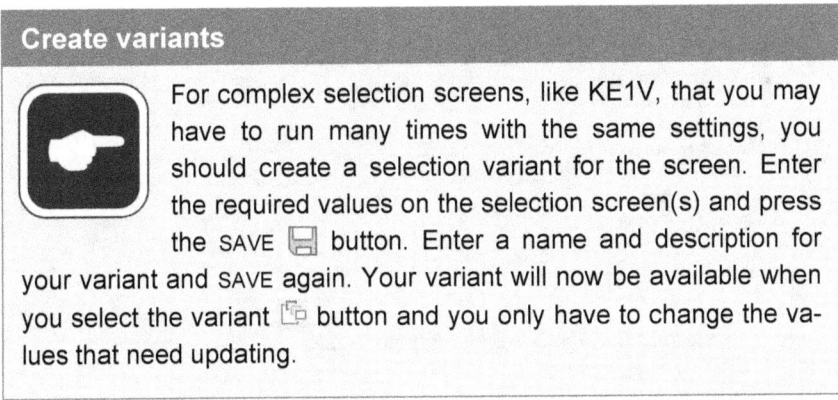

Figure 3.9: KE1V select value fields

When you get to the last screen, you see an EXECUTE button to perform the transfer. Back on the initial screen, you had a TEST RUN option which determined whether the execute option will perform the real transfer or a test transfer.

Create variants

For complex selection screens, like KE1V, that you may have to run many times with the same settings, you should create a selection variant for the screen. Enter the required values on the selection screen(s) and press the SAVE button. Enter a name and description for your variant and SAVE again. Your variant will now be available when you select the variant button and you only have to change the values that need updating.

After transferring the data, you can run the profit center plan line item report KE5Y to see the planned data that was transferred from COPA (see Figure 3.10).

63

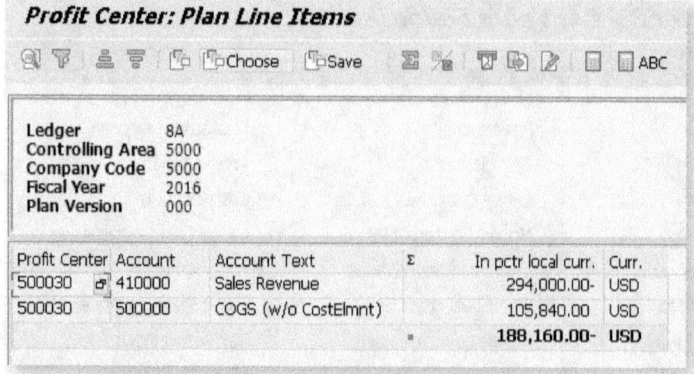

Figure 3.10: Plan line items transferred from COPA

3.4 Integrated cost planning

As you have seen, the plan data transfer from COPA is transferred periodically through the KE1V transaction. For overhead cost planning, you have the option to transfer the plan data in real time from cost objects such as cost centers, internal orders, or projects. The online transfer of data to PCA is activated in the plan version under SETTINGS FOR PROFIT CENTER ACCOUNTING (see Figure 3.11).

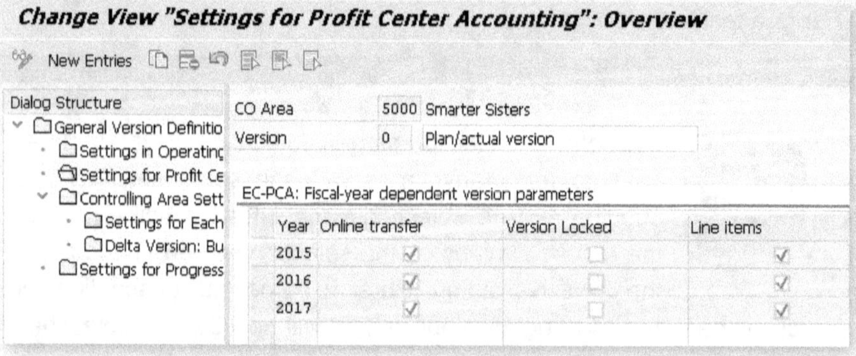

Figure 3.11: Setting for online transfer in plan version

You also need to set the indicator for INTEGRATED PLANNING in the planning version under CONTROLLING AREA SETTINGS • SETTINGS FOR EACH FISCAL YEAR (see Figure 3.12).

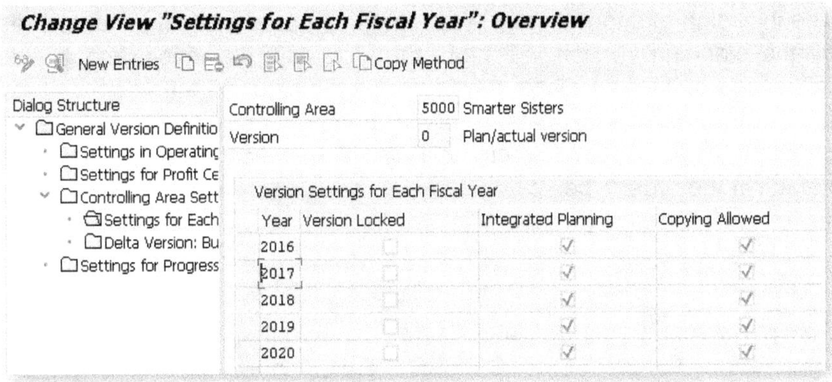

Figure 3.12: Setting for integrated planning

With these indicators set, cost object planning data, such as cost center plans entered directly in planning transactions such as KP06 (see Figure 3.13) or uploaded through the flexible Microsoft Excel upload function, will flow to PCA.

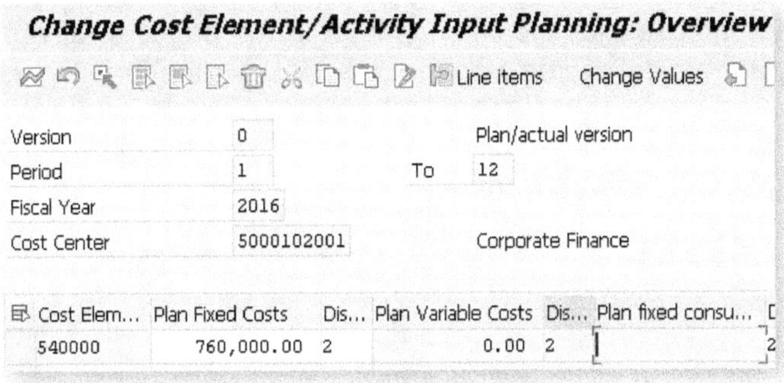

Figure 3.13: KP06 enter a cost center plan

You can now see the planned cost center values in PCA (see Figure 3.14).

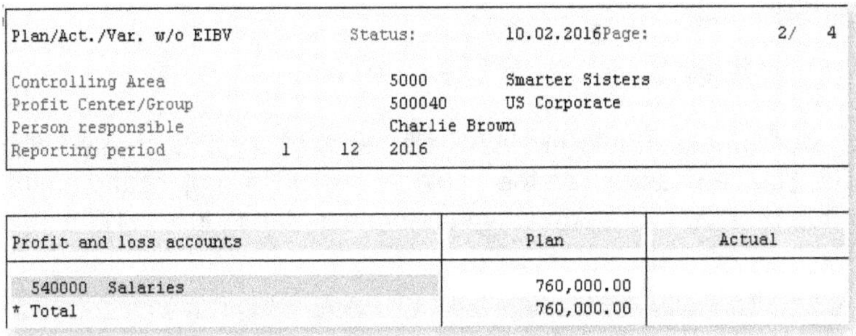

Figure 3.14: Cost center values transferred to PCA

The inclusion of internal order plans into integrated planning is controlled by the planning version indicators that you saw previously and is also influenced by the PLAN-INTEGRATED ORDER indicator on the CONTROL DATA tab of the order master data. If this indicator is not set, then the internal order plan will not flow directly to PCA. This indicator can be set as a default in the order type.

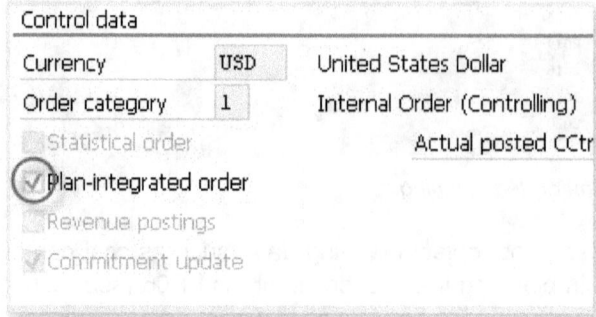

Figure 3.15: Plan integrated order

There is a similar indicator for projects, defined in the project profile in the configuration for project systems on the CONTROLLING tab (see Figure 3.16).

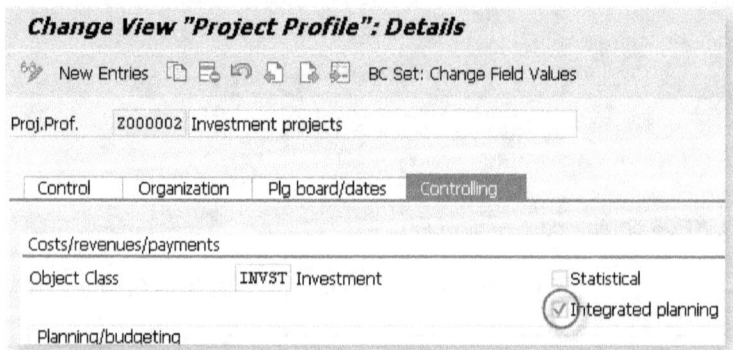

Figure 3.16: Integrated planning on the project profile

This indicator is passed into the WBS elements of projects created with this profile. You can see this on the CONTROL tab of the project and on the CONTROL tab of each WBS element in the project (see Figure 3.17).

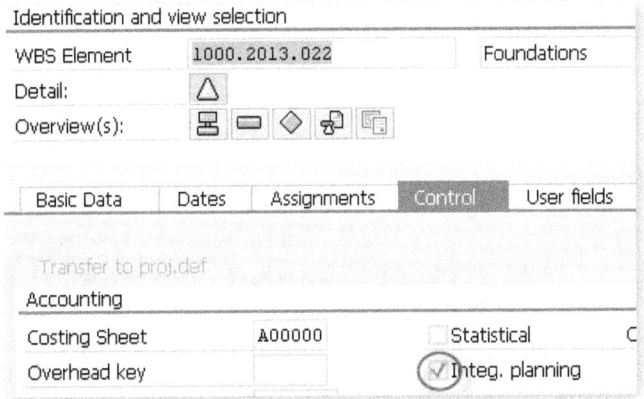

Figure 3.17: Integrated plan indicator on WBS element

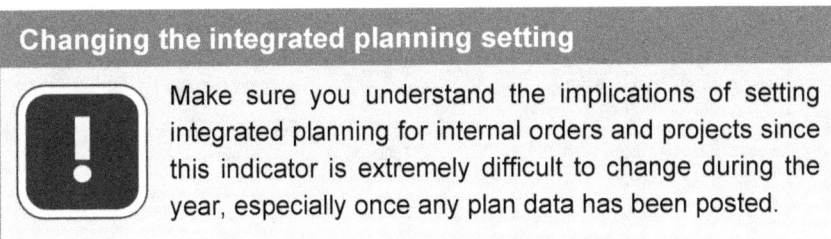

The plan integration does not only include direct primary cost planning, but also planned allocations such as activity planning, planned distributions, and planned assessments.

Activities can be used to represent a service provided by one cost object to other cost objects. For example, an IT service cost center may have a pool of hours that it wants to charge out to internal customer cost centers that require IT support. The number of hours and the charge-out rates are defined in activity planning for the sending cost center, transaction KP26 (see Figure 3.18). By planning both the activity rate and the quantity, the sending cost center receives a plan credit posting using the allocation cost element defined in the activity type. This is also reflected online in the profit center assigned to the sending cost center (see Figure 3.19).

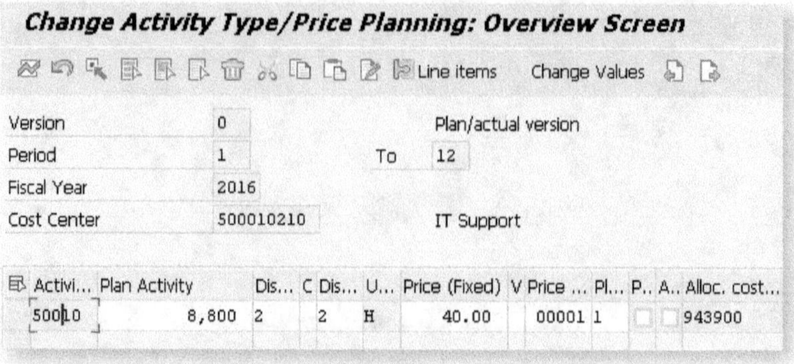
Change Activity Type/Price Planning: Overview Screen
Line items
Change Values
Version
0
Plan/actual version
Period
1
To
12
Fiscal Year
2016
Cost Center
500010210
IT Support
Activi... Plan Activity Dis... C Dis... U... Price (Fixed) V Price ... Pl... P.. A.. Alloc. cost...
50010 8,800 2 2 H 40.00 00001 1 943900

Figure 3.18: Activity price planning for cost center

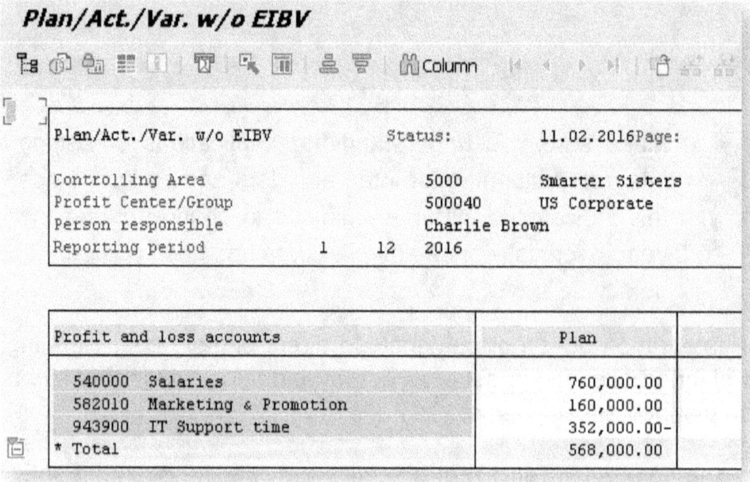
Plan/Act./Var. w/o EIBV
Column
Plan/Act./Var. w/o EIBV Status: 11.02.2016Page:
Controlling Area 5000 Smarter Sisters
Profit Center/Group 500040 US Corporate
Person responsible Charlie Brown
Reporting period 1 12 2016
Profit and loss accounts
Plan
540000 Salaries 760,000.00
582010 Marketing & Promotion 160,000.00
943900 IT Support time 352,000.00-
* Total 568,000.00

Figure 3.19: IT support credit in PCA plan

In cost center planning, internal customers also need to plan the quantity of the service that they are planning to consume in the year. This is done in KP06 using a layout that supports activity input planning (see Figure 3.20). The cost of the activity is reflected in the customer cost center and its related profit center online (see Figure 3.21).

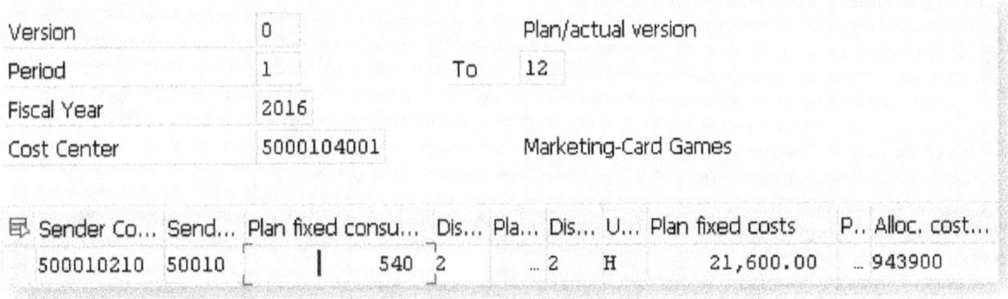

Version	0		Plan/actual version	
Period	1	To	12	
Fiscal Year	2016			
Cost Center	5000104001		Marketing-Card Games	

Sender Co...	Send...	Plan fixed consu...	Dis...	Pla...	Dis...	U...	Plan fixed costs	P..	Alloc. cost...
500010210	50010		540	2	... 2	H	21,600.00		... 943900

Figure 3.20: Activity input planning in cost center

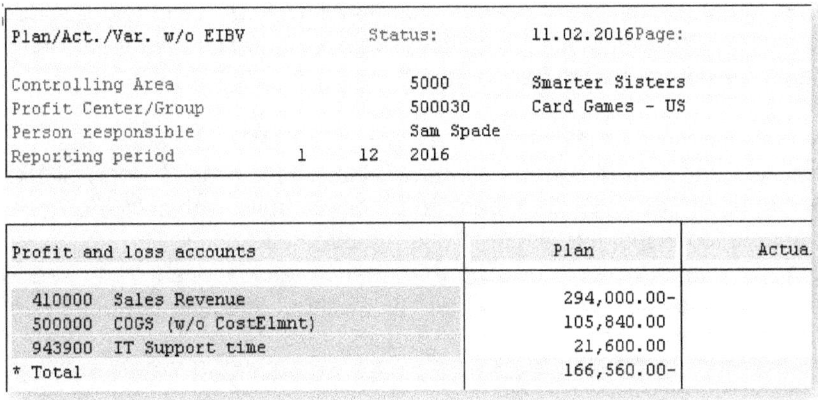

```
Plan/Act./Var. w/o EIBV          Status:      11.02.2016Page:

Controlling Area                 5000         Smarter Sisters
Profit Center/Group              500030       Card Games - US
Person responsible                            Sam Spade
Reporting period           1     12           2016
```

Profit and loss accounts	Plan	Actua
410000 Sales Revenue	294,000.00-	
500000 COGS (w/o CostElmnt)	105,840.00	
943900 IT Support time	21,600.00	
* Total	166,560.00-	

Figure 3.21: Activity input transferred to PCA online

Assessment and *distribution* are forms of allocation that work in a similar manner to move costs between cost objects. The major difference is that controlling assessment uses a secondary cost element to move the costs while distribution moves the cost using the original primary cost element. Running planned assessments or distributions moves the costs between the cost objects defined in the *cycle* and posts planned data online to PCA planning. For example, the assessment of planned costs from the human resources cost center will result in planned costs in the receiving profit centers if the cost centers in the assessment cross the profit center boundaries (see Figure 3.22). Planned distribution will have the same result, but uses different cost elements.

Profit and loss accounts		Plan	Actual
410000	Sales Revenue	294,000.00-	
500000	COGS (w/o CostElmnt)	105,840.00	
942500	Shared HR Costs	45,699.92	
943900	IT Support time	21,600.00	
* Total		120,860.08-	

Figure 3.22: Result of cost center planned assessment in PCA

Other forms of planned allocation also flow into PCA, including planned overhead calculations using a costing sheet, planned template allocation, and planned settlements from orders or projects.

Manual planning functions in PCA, discussed later on, show that assessment and distribution are also available. These are PCA-only allocations and will not pass data back to other controlling objects. For most planned allocations, it is better to use the overhead controlling options to integrate with PCA. Only use the PCA manual allocations if you need to make allocations at the profit center level without affecting the other controlling modules.

Depreciation and interest simulation from asset accounting can also flow into PCA by way of cost center planning. Running the depreciation/interest simulation transaction S_ALR_87099918 (see Figure 3.23) will post planned depreciation from asset accounting and investment management objects to cost center planning and through online integration into PCA (see Figure 3.24).

Report year: 2016 Primary Cost Planning: Depreciation/Interest - 01 Book depre
Date created: 11.02.2016 Periods 001-012 - Version 0 - Test run

	ObTyp	Object	Description	Per.ovh.01	Per.ovh.02	Per.ovh.03	Per.ovh.04
	AN			14,880.95	14,880.95	14,880.96	14,880.95
*		Cost element 640000		14,880.95	14,880.95	14,880.96	14,880.95
**		Activity Type		14,880.95	14,880.95	14,880.96	14,880.95
***		Cost Center 5000101100		14,880.95	14,880.95	14,880.96	14,880.95
	OR			0.00	0.00	5,555.56	5,555.55
*		Cost element 640000		0.00	0.00	5,555.56	5,555.55

Figure 3.23: Planned depreciation

```
Plan/Act./Var. w/o EIBV         Status:       11.02.2016Page:

Controlling Area                              5000          Smarter Sisters
Profit Center/Group                           500050        Manufacturing
Person responsible                            Bob Builder
Reporting period              1      12       2016
```

Profit and loss accounts	Plan	Actua
540000 Salaries	4,280,000.00	
640000 Depreciation Expense	234,126.99	
942500 Shared HR Costs	703,780.08	
* Total	5,217,907.07	

Figure 3.24: Depreciation plan flows in PCA

In the end, you can choose whether to have online plan integration active between the other controlling objects and PCA. If you decide against online integration, you can transfer plans from the objects to profit center planning periodically by using transaction 1KE0 (see Figure 3.25). You can choose the objects to transfer and you can also choose values and groups for plan transfer.

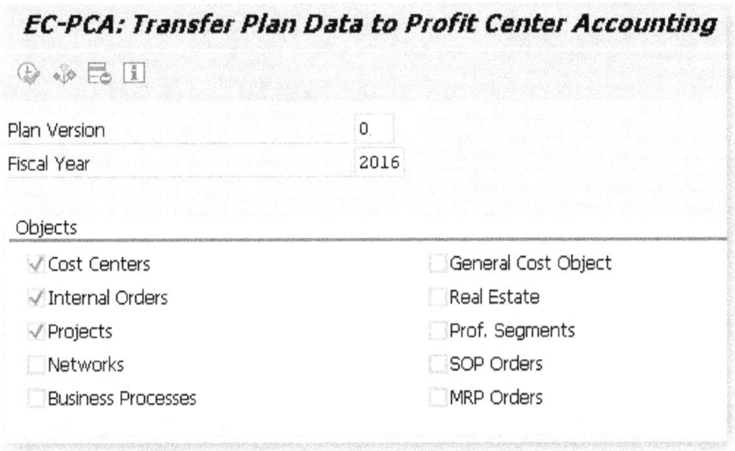

EC-PCA: Transfer Plan Data to Profit Center Accounting

Plan Version	0
Fiscal Year	2016

Objects

✓ Cost Centers	☐ General Cost Object
✓ Internal Orders	☐ Real Estate
✓ Projects	☐ Prof. Segments
☐ Networks	☐ SOP Orders
☐ Business Processes	☐ MRP Orders

Figure 3.25: Plan transfer to PCA

3.5   Statistical key figure planning

You can transfer cost plans online from cost objects into PCA and you can also have statistical key figure planning integrate online. If your SKF has been maintained in configuration in transaction 3KEG (refer back to

Figure 2.24) then the SKF values planned on an internal order or a cost center (see Figure 3.26) will also appear in PCA planning (see Figure 3.27).

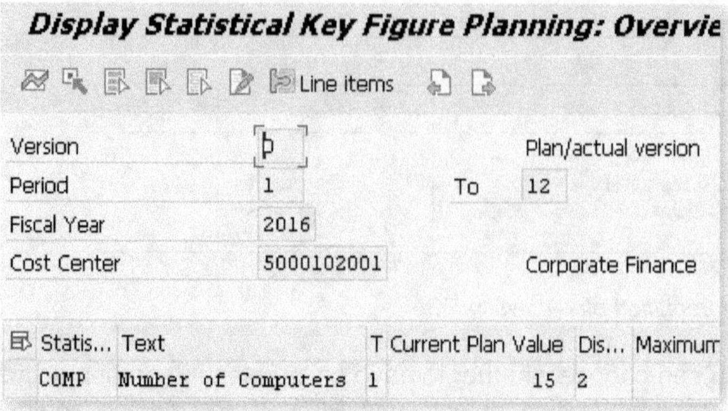

```
Display Statistical Key Figure Planning: Overvie
   ⊠ ⓠ 🖹 🖹 🖹 📝 📋 Line items   ⬇ ⬆

 Version              [ p ]           Plan/actual version
 Period               1          To   12
 Fiscal Year          2016
 Cost Center          5000102001      Corporate Finance

 📋 Statis... Text                  T Current Plan Value Dis... Maximum
    COMP  Number of Computers   1                  15   2
```

Figure 3.26: Cost center SKF plan

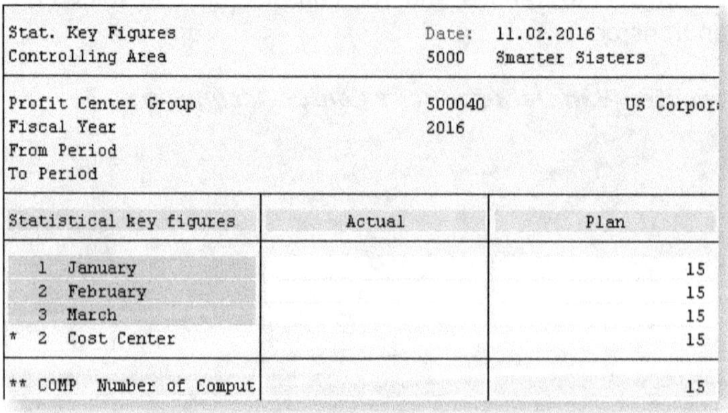

```
Stat. Key Figures              Date:    11.02.2016
Controlling Area                        5000    Smarter Sisters

Profit Center Group                     500040            US Corpor:
Fiscal Year                             2016
From Period
To Period

Statistical key figures      Actual              Plan

    1  January                                            15
    2  February                                           15
    3  March                                              15
 *  2  Cost Center                                        15

 ** COMP  Number of Comput                                15
```

Figure 3.27: SKF transferred to PCA plan

As with the other planned values, you can activate online integration for planned SKFs. If you decide not to activate an online transfer, you can use transaction 1KEE to transfer planned SKF values periodically (see Figure 3.28).

SKFs can also be planned manually in PCA, which is touched upon in the next section.

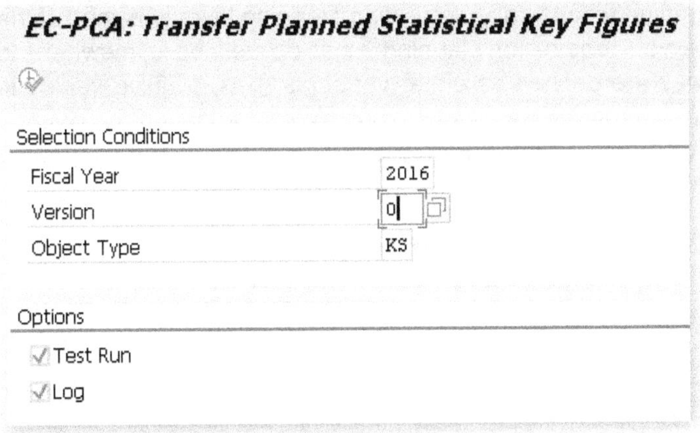

```
EC-PCA: Transfer Planned Statistical Key Figures

Selection Conditions
    Fiscal Year                    2016
    Version                        0
    Object Type                    KS

Options
    ✓ Test Run
    ✓ Log
```

Figure 3.28: Transfer planned SKF to PCA

3.6 Manual planning in classic PCA

While it is definitely a good practice to integrate your planning as much as you can, there may be situations where manual planning functions in profit center accounting are useful or even necessary. One example would be planning balance sheet values that cannot be transferred from any other module. There may also be organizations that do not use CO-PA planning and would then plan revenue and costs manually in PCA. Finally, there may be costs in your P&L that you do not assign to a controlling object or associate with a cost element. These items should also be planned manually in PCA.

In order to manually enter plan data into SAP, you first need to have a *planning layout* defined and a *planner profile* assigned to your user. SAP provides a number of predefined planning layouts and planner profiles, but you can also create your own in configuration. (I am often asked to build a monthly planning layout for businesses so that they can populate their plans in a spreadsheet and then upload them into SAP Planning.)

Specific layouts must exist for any objects that require manual planning. In PCA, there are different sets of layouts for balance sheet accounts, revenue, costs, and statistical key figures. The layouts are created and edited using the *report painter* functionality in SAP. Once you have created a planning layout, you need to assign it to a planner profile before you can use it.

The important thing to know about creating planning layouts is that all the characteristics you require for planning must be defined somewhere in the layout. They are defined as either variables, sets, or fixed values in the lead columns (see Figure 3.29) in your layout, defined in the general data section of the report (see Figure 3.30), or used in one of the key figure columns (see Figure 3.31).

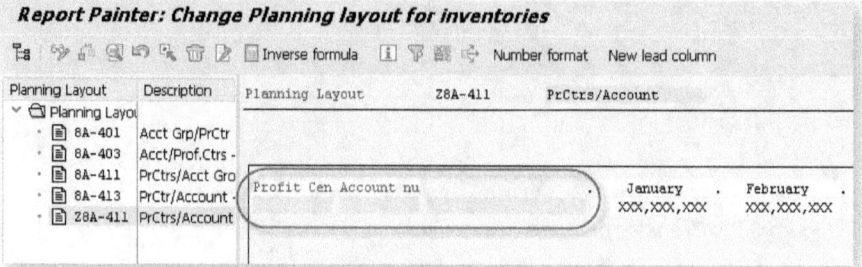

Figure 3.29: Planning layout lead columns

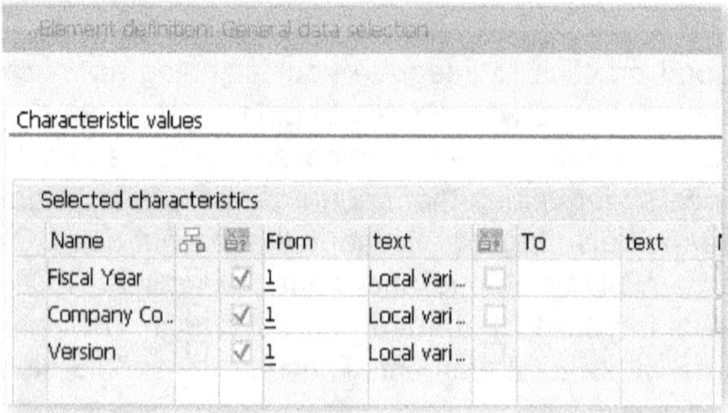

Figure 3.30: Planning layout general data selection

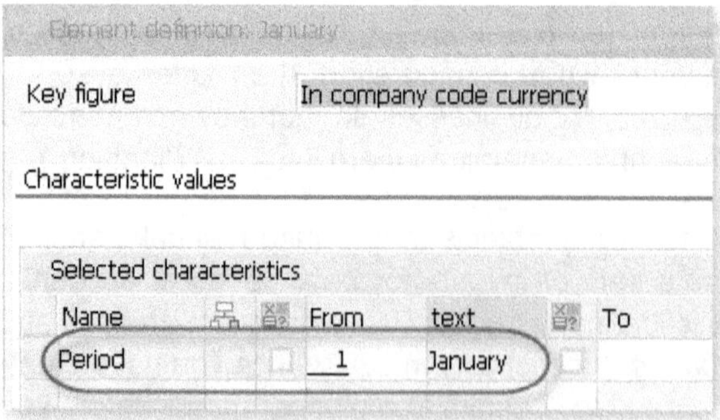

Figure 3.31: Characteristic assigned to key figure

Once defined, the layout needs to be assigned to a planner profile in configuration (see Figure 3.32).

> ### Create your own planner profile
>
>  SAP advises against modifying standard delivered planner profiles if possible. If you are going to be making your own planning layouts and adding them to planner profiles, it is advisable to copy the SAP delivered profiles that you need and adjust and use those.

Figure 3.32: Assign layout to planner profile

Here, you also have an INTEGRATED check box. This does not have anything to do with integrated planning; instead, this activates Excel in your planning layout. With integrated Excel, you open your planning layout in an Excel worksheet layout rather than in a standard planning screen. Integrated Excel is also the starting point for creating the file descriptions and templates to be used in a flexible Excel upload of plan data. This function is generic across CO modules and can be used for all planning functions for cost centers, internal orders, statistical key figures, activity types, COPA, and more.

Since this function can be so useful, it is worth showing the steps in detail. The first step is to check the integrated Excel box associated with your planning layout. Next, select the layout and go to the DEFAULT PARAMETERS sub-dialog and enter some selection variables (see Figure 3.33). It is better to run this with the following option selected: ● Form-Based. Select the OVERVIEW button to open the layout in an Excel format. You will receive a message about the file description being generated and then you see the layout in Excel (see Figure 3.34). You may have to accept macros or otherwise change some security settings in Excel if it does not open immediately.

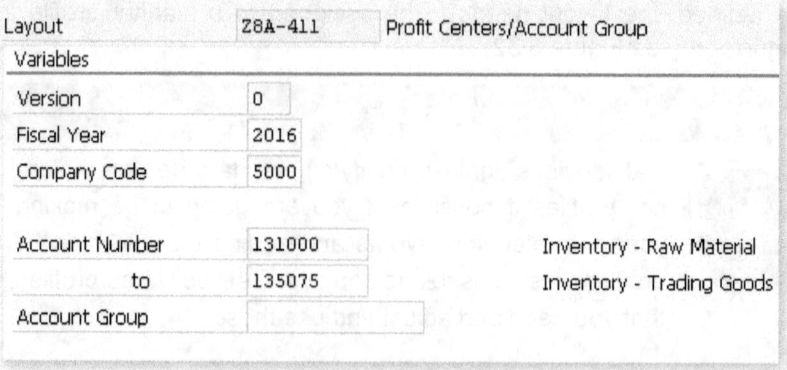
Layout
Z8A-411
Profit Centers/Account Group
Variables
Version
0
Fiscal Year
2016
Company Code
5000
Account Number
131000
Inventory - Raw Material
to
135075
Inventory - Trading Goods
Account Group

Figure 3.33: Enter parameters

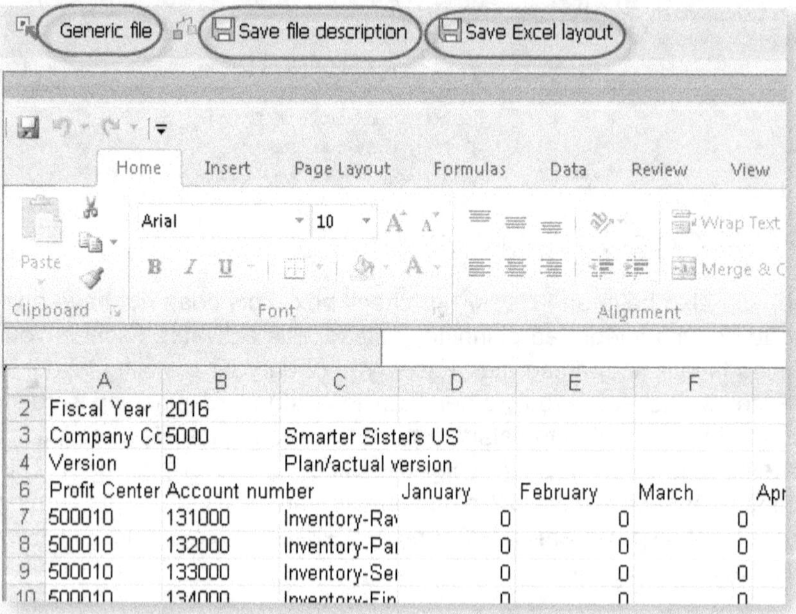
Generic file
Save file description
Save Excel layout
Home
Insert
Page Layout
Formulas
Data
Review
View
Arial
10
Wrap Text
Paste
Merge & C
Clipboard
Font
Alignment
Fiscal Year 2016
Company Cc 5000 Smarter Sisters US
Version 0 Plan/actual version
Profit Center Account number January February March Apr
500010 131000 Inventory-Ra 0 0 0
500010 132000 Inventory-Pa 0 0 0
500010 133000 Inventory-Se 0 0 0

Figure 3.34: Microsoft Excel layout

You will notice three buttons in the layout. The first is used to generate a generic file. This is the link between the physical file and the generated file description. In uploading files, the system looks for files containing the generic file name. The generic file should consist of a fixed part which will be common to all the physical files to be imported and then a "*" representing a variable portion and the file extension which may be .txt or .csv (see Figure 3.35).

Figure 3.35: Generic file name

To complete the process, click on the SAVE FILE DESCRIPTION button and then on the SAVE EXCEL LAYOUT button. Use the FILE • SAVE AS or the [F12] key in the Excel sheet to save a template copy of the layout locally. When you back out of the layout and the parameter screen, it is not necessary to save the default parameters unless you want them to appear as defaults in manual planning. When you go back to the layout view, you should now see the file description linked to the planning layout (see Figure 3.36).

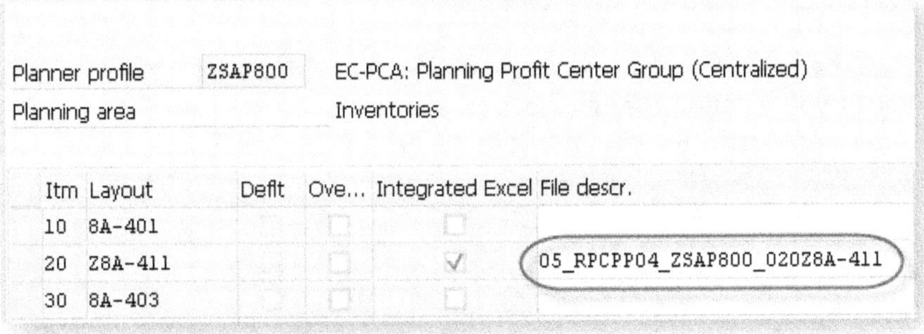

Figure 3.36: File description on the planning layout

You can use the template that you saved locally to fill with planned values and upload into SAP. You have to unprotect the spreadsheet and remove any total rows that have been inserted by SAP. To upload, first populate the file with plan data and save as either a .txt or .csv file, depending on what you selected previously in the generic file. Next, use the UPLOAD FROM EXCEL transaction 7KEX to import your plan (see Figure 3.37). You have the option to upload a single file or all files in a directory. SAP will look for all files in the directory containing the generic file name and will import them. You also have to select the FILE DESCRIPTION associated with your layout. There may be multiple options available, so it is important to select the correct file description. It must be the same as the one generated (as seen in Figure 3.36).

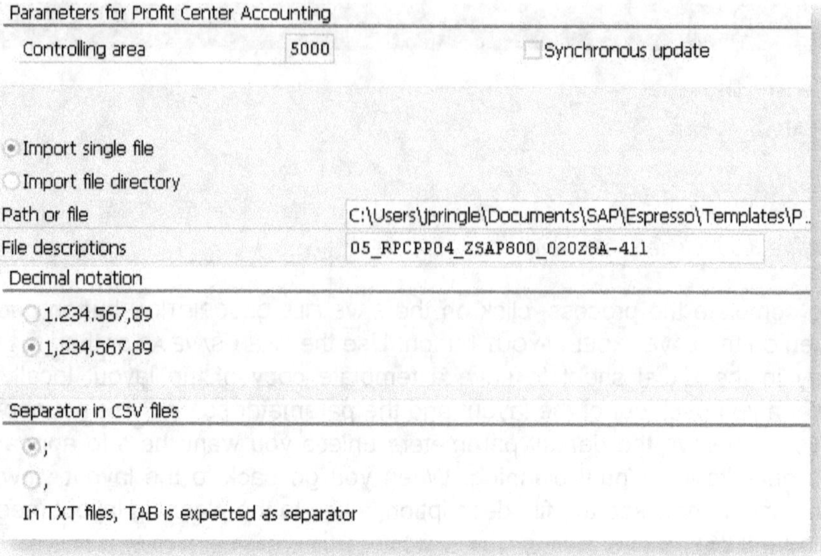

PLANNING IN CLASSIC PCA

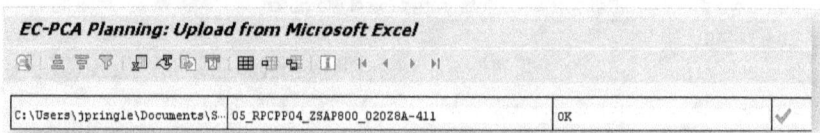

Figure 3.37: Upload from Microsoft Excel

Execute the upload by pressing the 🕒 button. There will be a message telling you whether the upload was successful or not (see Figure 3.38) and if successful, the planned data will be in PCA (see Figure 3.39).

Figure 3.38: Upload message

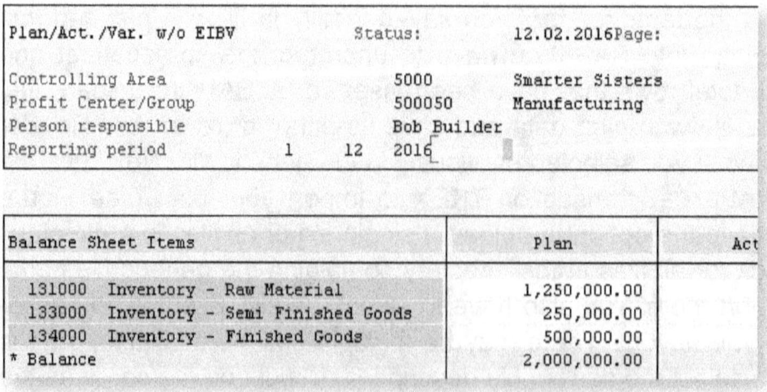

Figure 3.39: Balance sheet plan uploaded from Excel

> **If you have problems with the upload**
>
>  There is a lot of useful information on possible issues that might cause errors in an Excel upload contained in SAP note 319713—Error with Excel upload—possible causes. If you get an error message with your upload, this note will likely explain the underlying issue. This note also outlines what you need to do if you make changes to a layout and need to regenerate the file layout and the generic file name.

Manual planning can also be entered directly into SAP using either a standard layout or an Excel integrated layout. It is possible to enter manual plans directly for costs, revenues, balance sheet accounts, and statistical key figures. As mentioned, these plans only affect PCA and do not integrate back to any other modules. The relevant transactions are:

- 7KE1 and 7KE2 for cost and revenue planning
- 7KE3 and 7KE4 for balance sheet planning
- 7KE5 and 7KE6 for statistical key figure planning

The basic concepts are the same for each, so I only demonstrate cost and revenue planning manually. In the example company, there are a number of expense accounts that are not under the direct control of any of the cost center managers, so you want to manually plan these at the profit center level. On the initial screen, (Figure 3.40), enter the selection criteria for the plan.

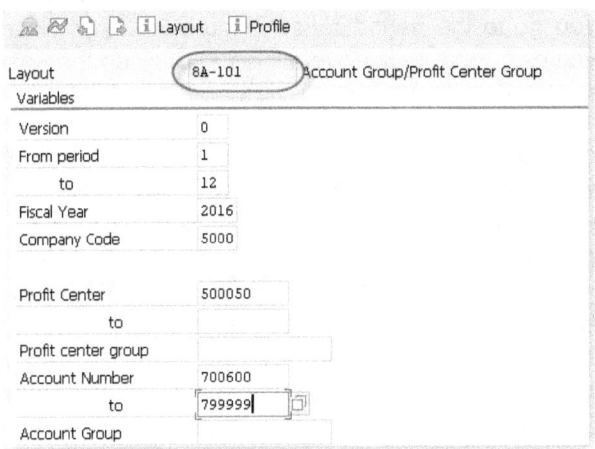

Figure 3.40: Cost and revenue planning initial screen

79

The selection criteria and the values on the following planning screen are controlled by the planning layout that you are using. If there are multiple planning layouts linked to your planner profile, you can toggle through them using the FORWARD and BACK buttons. Next, go into the planning screen (Figure 3.41) by pressing the OVERVIEW button or alternatively press the PERIOD SCREEN button to plan at an individual period level.

Change Plan Costs/Revenues: Cumulative values

Fiscal Year	2016		
Period	1	To	12
Company Code	5000		Smarter Sisters US
Version	0		Plan/actual version
Account Number	701000		Extraordinary Expenses / Ir

Profit center	Text	PrCtr report cur.	Distri...	U...
500050	Manufacturing	240,000.00	7	

Figure 3.41: Enter planning data

As mentioned, the appearance of this screen is controlled by the layout that was chosen. When planning at the overview level you have the chance to select a *distribution key*. This determines how the plan is distributed to the periods in your selection. Key 7 distributes the overall value to the periods based on the number of days in the period. Other distribution keys are available and additional keys can be added in the configuration. When you go to the periodic view (Figure 3.42), you can also enter or change values to update the overall value. Click on the post button to update the plan data in the system.

It is useful to note how balance sheet planning works in PCA for both direct manual planning and file upload. Balance sheet plan entries are treated as cumulative values when they are originally posted to SAP. For example, when you posted planned values for inventory through your upload file, it contained a value in each period (see Figure 3.43). Displaying the plan for the balance sheet at any period displays that cumulative amount and not the sum of all the preceding periods. So by showing a balance sheet for periods 1 to 4, you see $500,000 in the inventory plan instead of $2,000,000 (see Figure 3.44).

P...	Text	PrCtr report cur.	Unit
1	January	20,327.87	USD
2	February	19,016.39	USD
3	March	20,327.87	USD
4	April	19,672.13	USD
5	May	20,327.87	USD
6	June	19,672.13	USD
7	July	20,327.87	USD
8	August	20,327.87	USD
9	September	19,672.13	USD
10	October	20,327.87	USD
11	November	19,672.13	USD
12	December	20,327.87	USD
*Pe		240,000.00	

Figure 3.42: Periodic view of planning

	A	B	C	D	E	F	G	H	I
2	Fiscal Year	2016							
3	Company	Cc5000	Smarter Sisters US						
4	Version	0	Plan/actual version						
5	Profit Center	Account number		January	February	March	April	May	June
7	500050	134000	Inventory-Fin	500000	500000	500000	500000	500000	500000
8	Profit Cen	134000	Inventory-Fin	500000	500000	500000	500000	500000	500000

Figure 3.43: Entry of planned balance sheet values

```
Plan/Act./Var. w/o EIBV       Status:        17.02.2016 Page:

Controlling Area              5000           Smarter Sisters
Profit Center/Group           500050         Manufacturing
Person responsible            Bob Builder
Reporting period        1   4 2016
```

Balance Sheet Items	Plan	Actu
134000 Inventory - Finished Goods	500,000.00	
* Balance	500,000.00	

Figure 3.44: Display planned inventory periods 1 to 4

Manually making changes to one of these cumulative values will post plan lines that reflect the change values and will not repost the cumulative amounts. For example, as shown in Figure 3.45, change the inventory value in April to $550,000.

PLANNING IN CLASSIC PCA

	A	B	C	D	E	F	G	H	I
2	Fiscal Year	2016							
3	Company	Cc5000	Smarter Sisters US						
4	Version	0	Plan/actual version						
6	Profit Center	Account number		January	February	March	April	May	June
7	500050	134000	Inventory-Fin	500000	500000	500000	550000	500000	500000
8	Profit Cen	134000	Inventory-Fin	500000	500000	500000	500000	500000	500000

Figure 3.45: Change cumulative value in plan

The profit center plan line items show the original $500,000 posting then an increase of $50,000 in April and then a decrease as the value returns to $500,000 in May (see Figure 3.46).

Ledger	8A
Controlling Area	5000
Company Code	5000
Fiscal Year	2016
Plan Version	000

Profit Center	Account	Account Text	Σ	In pctr local curr.	Curr.
500050	134000	Inventory-FinGoods		500,000.00	USD
500050	134000	Inventory-FinGoods		50,000.00	USD
500050	134000	Inventory-FinGoods		50,000.00-	USD
				500,000.00	**USD**

Figure 3.46: PCA line items for balance sheet change

If you want to carry forward the balance sheet plan closing values into the following planning year, you can run transaction 7KES. Depending on your SAP release, you may have to allow the carry forward in PCA using transaction 2KET before you can do this.

You can also do planned assessments and distributions directly in PCA using the transactions 3KEB – Assessment, or 4KEB – Distribution. These allocations are set up and behave in a way similar to the cost center allocations that you are familiar with. As with the cost center allocations, you must use a secondary cost element for assessment while distribution uses the original cost elements.

> **Planned allocation**
>
>  Perform the planned allocation between CO objects first, using integrated planning to achieve most of the planned PCA allocations that you require. Only use PCA planned allocations to move any costs not touched by the CO allocations.

In most areas of planning in SAP, there are transactions to enable you to copy data into plans. In classic PCA, this transaction is 7KEV. Within this transaction, it is possible to copy data a variety of ways:

▶ Actual to plan
▶ Plan to plan—different versions or the same version in different periods/years
▶ Revaluations with the copy
▶ Add versus overwrite in the target plan

In the 7KEV initial screen (see Figure 3.47), there are a number of sections to define the copy parameters. ❶ The PLANNING AREA—where you select either costs/revenues, balance sheet accounts or statistical key figures. ❷ The COPY FROM parameters where you select the RECORD TYPE as actual, plan, actual assessment/distribution, planned assessment distribution or year-end closing posting. Here, you also select the VERSION, COMPANY CODE, and FISCAL YEAR to copy from. ❸ In the COPY TO section, you define the VERSION, COMPANY CODE, and FISCAL YEAR to receive the copy. ❹ This section allows you to select the PERIODS for the transfer. In this way, you can do a partial copy with actual data and then complete the year by copying plan data from another version. ❺ Here you can choose to apply a REVALUATION FACTOR to the plan data being copied, such as increase the plan by 5%. For complex plan revaluation, you can define a *user exit* and link it here. ❻ Finally, you can decide what will happen with EXISTING PLAN DATA; will it be added to or overwritten.

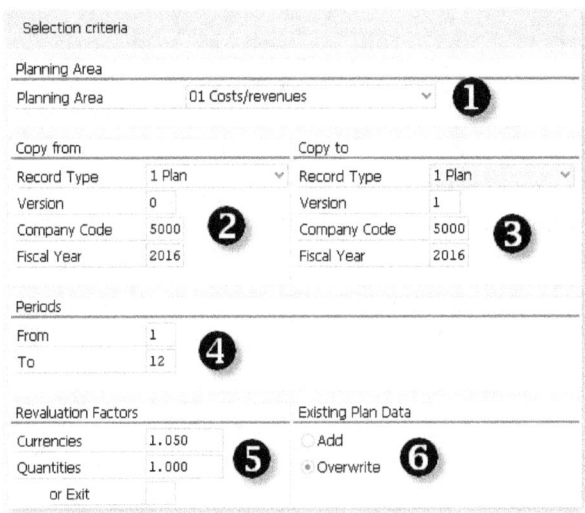

Figure 3.47: Copy planning initial screen

After completing the parameters in Figure 3.47, click on the SELECTION CRITERIA button to make the selections of objects for the copy (see Figure 3.48). Copy the revenue plan for group 50001 with a 5% revaluation from version 0 to version 1 (see Figure 3.49).

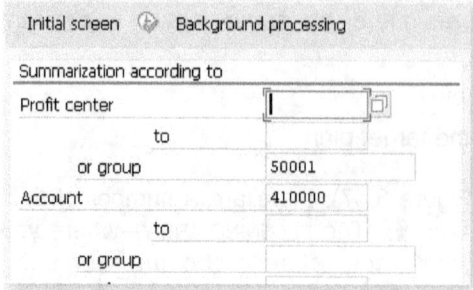

Figure 3.48: Selection for plan copy

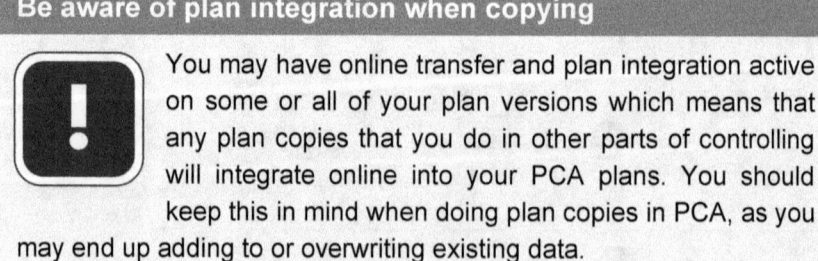

Figure 3.49: Results of plan copy

You could run the copy several times to revalue different groups of accounts at different rates or have a user exit built to address that requirement.

Be aware of plan integration when copying

You may have online transfer and plan integration active on some or all of your plan versions which means that any plan copies that you do in other parts of controlling will integrate online into your PCA plans. You should keep this in mind when doing plan copies in PCA, as you may end up adding to or overwriting existing data.

It is also possible to use *formula planning* in PCA. This allows you to generate planned values based on formulas defined in *templates*. Templates are sophisticated calculation tools primarily used in the *activity*

Planning in classic PCA

based costing component in SAP, but are also available for planning in both cost center accounting and PCA.

As an example, next is a rather simple template which will calculate planned values based on some formulas involving statistical key figures. In the template shown in Figure 3.50, there are two calculation rows; one is related to revenue and the other is for calculating planned salary expense. For the revenue, simply multiply the planned value of an SKF called SALQTY—planned sales quantity by another SKF called AVEPRI—Average price. You can maintain the planned values for these in SKF planning manually. For the salary expense, multiply the SKF for headcount by another SKF for average salary in the profit center.

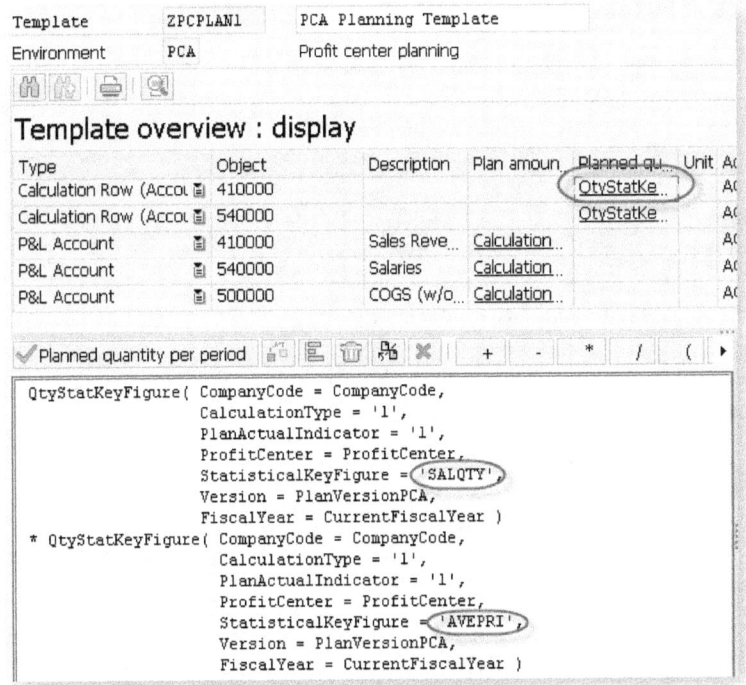

Figure 3.50: Template for PCA formula planning

Below the calculation rows are the P&L account rows. Reference the calculation rows and do some additional calculations. For example, for COGS account 500000, take the calculation row 410000 and multiply by 65% to give a value in the cost of sales line in the plan (see Figure 3.51).

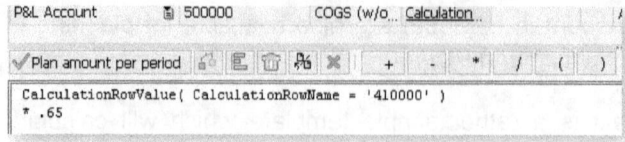

Figure 3.51: Cost of sales calculation in template

You can have similar lines for revenue and salaries where each references a calculation row. Note that you can use the same calculation row multiple times.

To use the template in formula planning, it is necessary to assign it to your profit centers. This is done on the profit center master on the INDICATORS tab (see Figure 3.52).

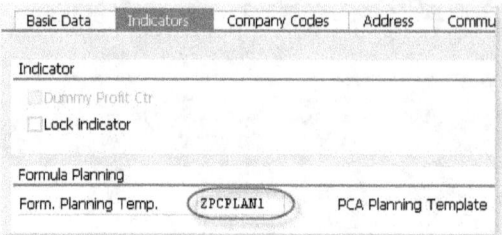

Figure 3.52: Assign a template to a profit center

You then need to execute transaction 7KET to generate formula planning (see Figure 3.53).

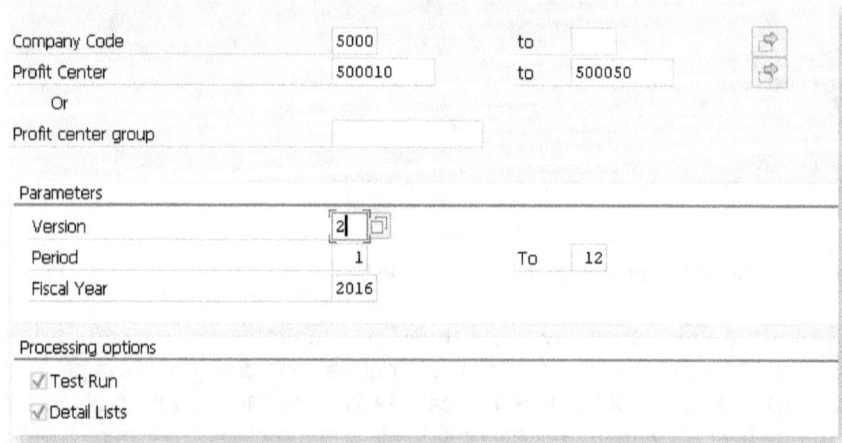

Figure 3.53: Execute formula planning

When you execute this, you see values in plan version 2 based on the formulas in your template (see Figure 3.54).

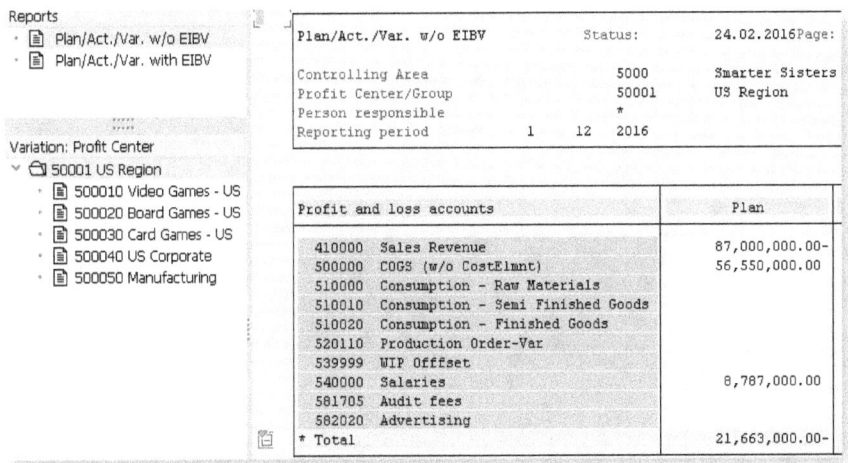

Figure 3.54: Results of formula planning

3.7 Summary

In this chapter, you learned how planning works in SAP classic PCA. You saw how PCA planning fits into an overall planning cycle that can include COPA planning, cost center and cost object planning, and sales and operations planning. You learned about the concept of versions in planning and how they are used throughout planning in SAP controlling. You learned about integrated planning and saw which settings allow plan data to flow from other SAP objects into PCA planning. You looked at planning for statistical key figures and how they can also be integrated with other controlling objects. Finally, you learned about manual planning in classic PCA and how to use techniques such as flexible Excel upload, plan copy functionality, and formula-based planning. In the next chapter, you see that many of the same concepts apply for profit center planning in the new GL.

4 Profit center planning in the new GL

In this chapter, I explain how profit center planning is carried out in the new general ledger. You will see the differences between classic PCA and profit center accounting in the new GL in online integration and manual planning.

4.1 How new GL planning fits

All the statements made about the planning cycle at the beginning of the last chapter still apply when you switch over to the new GL. The only difference is that the GL plan becomes the ultimate target for your integrated planning data (see Figure 4.1).

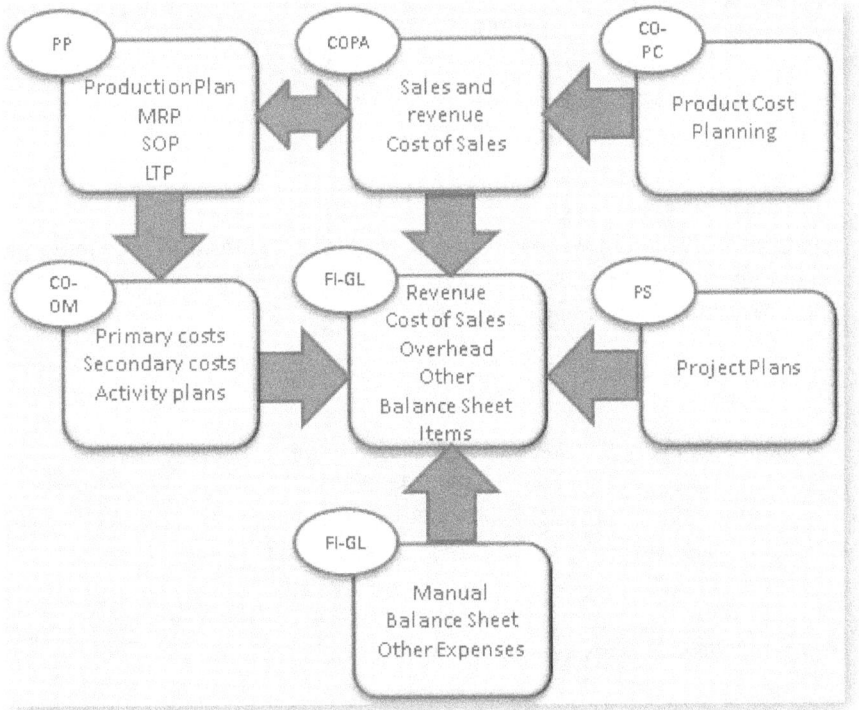

Figure 4.1: Generic planning cycle with new GL

89

4.2 Planning version concept in new GL

In addition to having the planning versions maintained in controlling, it is also necessary to configure planning versions in FI for GL planning. Functionally, these serve the same purpose as the planning versions in CO in that they allow multiple iterations of a plan stored in the system in parallel.

The basic settings for planning versions for the GL are set up in the SAP IMG under SAP CUSTOMIZING IMPLEMENTATION GUIDE • FINANCIAL ACCOUNTING (NEW) • GENERAL LEDGER ACCOUNTING (NEW) • PLANNING. First, you have to define plan periods (see Figure 4.2). This defines the periods allowed for planning and is tied to the posting period variant which is in turn linked to different company codes.

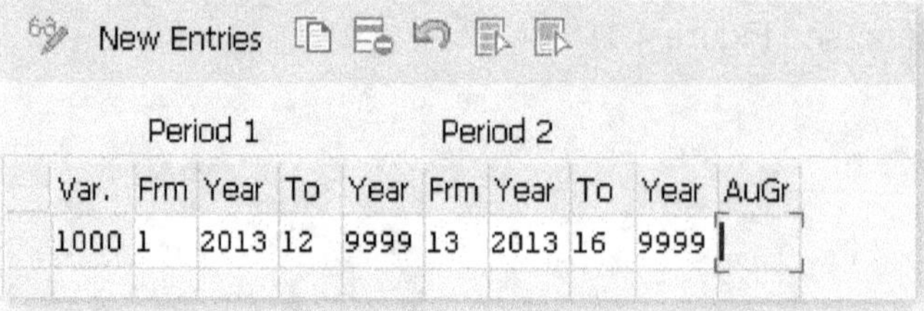

	Period 1			Period 2			
Var.	Frm Year	To	Year	Frm Year	To	Year	AuGr
1000	1 2013	12	9999	13 2013	16	9999	

Figure 4.2: Define plan periods for GL planning

Next, define the plan versions themselves (see Figure 4.3). For integrated planning and online transfers, you should define the same versions as you are going to use in CO.

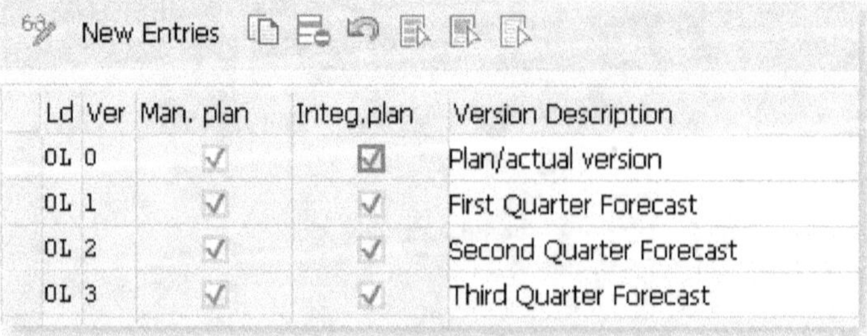

Ld	Ver	Man. plan	Integ.plan	Version Description
0L	0	✓	✓	Plan/actual version
0L	1	✓	✓	First Quarter Forecast
0L	2	✓	✓	Second Quarter Forecast
0L	3	✓	✓	Third Quarter Forecast

Figure 4.3: Plan versions for GL planning

One of the features introduced with the new GL is the ledger concept. This allows you to create different ledgers within FI to deal with parallel accounting requirements such as keeping records under two different accounting principles. It is possible to have plans in each ledger by assigning planning versions at the ledger level, but for simplicity I only show planning in the leading ledger. The first of the two check boxes allows manual planning in the version and the second specifies that plan data can be transferred from COPA and overhead cost controlling.

Next, define the fiscal-year-dependent parameters for the plan version (see Figure 4.4). These are set up specific to ledger, version, company code, and fiscal year. Here, you see the line item and opening balance check boxes, but you cannot access them. The check box values are set in the next step.

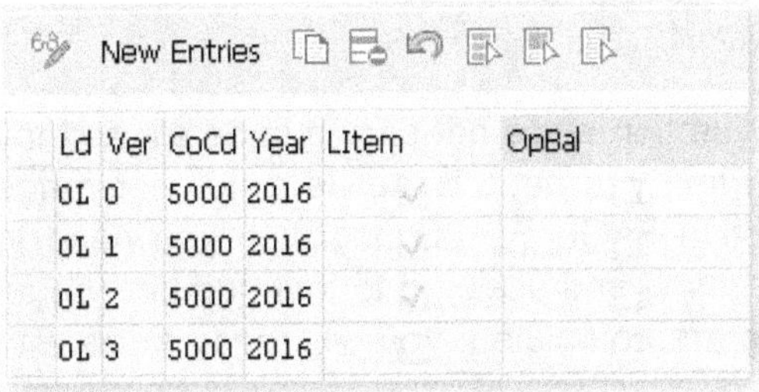

Ld	Ver	CoCd	Year	LItem	OpBal
0L	0	5000	2016	✓	
0L	1	5000	2016	✓	
0L	2	5000	2016	✓	
0L	3	5000	2016		

Figure 4.4: GL planning fiscal-year-dependent parameters

If you want to have plan line items written for all changes to the plan, you should set the line items indicator. If you are planning balance sheet items and you want the opening balance of the planned total records to also be stored as a line item, you should set the opening balance with the line item indicator. This is done by running the IMG transaction FAGLGCLE Activate line Items for planning (see Figure 4.5). If you complete the OPENING BALANCE section, you also want to set the opening balance with the line item indicator.

Ledger	0L
Version	3
Company Code	5000
Fiscal Year	2016
Opening Balance	
✓ Update opening balance	
Document type for beg. balance	P0

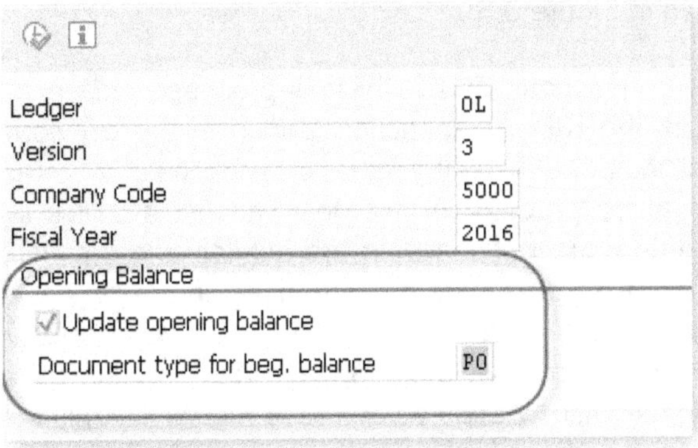

Figure 4.5: Activate update of plan line items

The result of running the update is shown in Figure 4.6 for plan version 3. Note the difference from Figure 4.4.

Ld	Ver	CoCd	Year	Locked	LItem	OpBal
OL	0	5000	2016	☐	✓	
OL	1	5000	2016	☐	✓	
OL	2	5000	2016	☐	✓	
OL	3	5000	2016	☐	✓	✓

Figure 4.6: After activation of line items

There are two additional configuration steps not shown in detail, as they are relatively straightforward. First, you need to define a number range for plan documents in transaction FAGL_PL_LC and then you need to define a document type for planning and assign it to that number range. After these configuration steps are completed, you are ready to go with GL planning.

4.3 Integrated revenue and COGS planning

As with classic PCA, the starting point for revenue and COGS planning should be COPA. After entering the planned sales quantities in the COPA planning framework and performing valuation, the planned values can be transferred to the new GL planning. Before this can happen, a mapping must be done between the COPA value fields and the GL accounts. Luckily, this is identical to what you did for the PCA transfer using the KEDP transaction (shown in Figure 3.5).

The transfer itself uses transaction KE1Z, which is processed in an almost identical fashion as the KE1V transaction shown in the previous chapter. There is an INITIAL SCREEN (see Figure 4.7) followed by three other screens that should be processed in order. The PROCESSING INSTRUCTION screen presents more options than are available in the PCA transfer, but the function is the same. The screen shown in Figure 4.8 is deliberately not showing all the available options. The SELECTION CRITERIA screen (see Figure 4.9) will also have more options, but it is simply a selection screen. Finally, the VALUE FIELDS screen (see Figure 4.10) is the same as for the PCA transfer. You simply pick the value field to transfer to the GL.

PROFIT CENTER PLANNING IN THE NEW GL

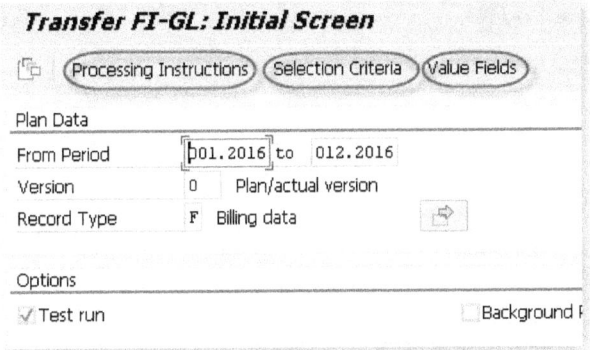

Figure 4.7: KE1Z Initial screen

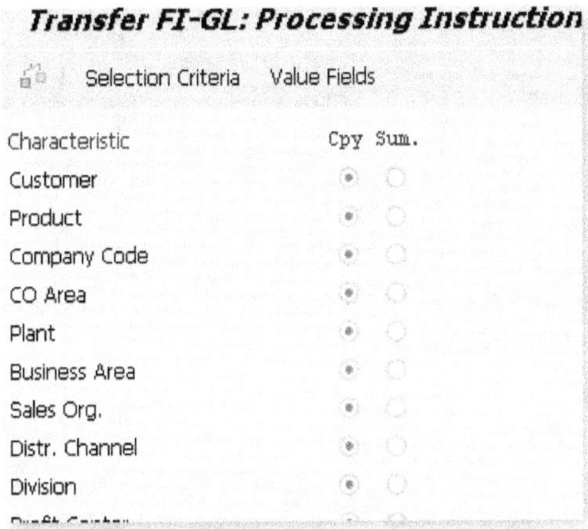

Figure 4.8: KE1Z processing instructions

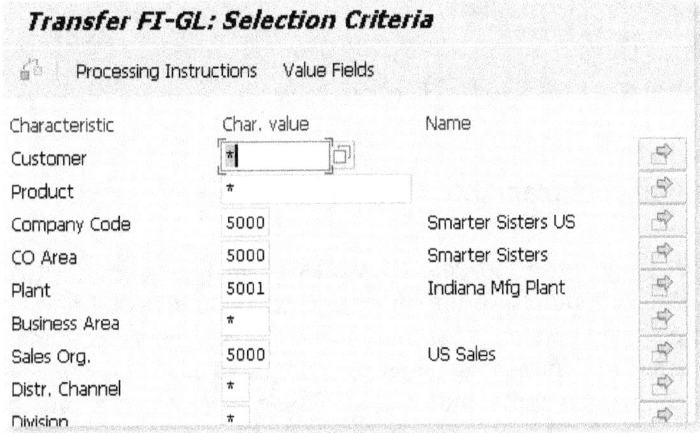

Figure 4.9: KE1Z selection criteria

93

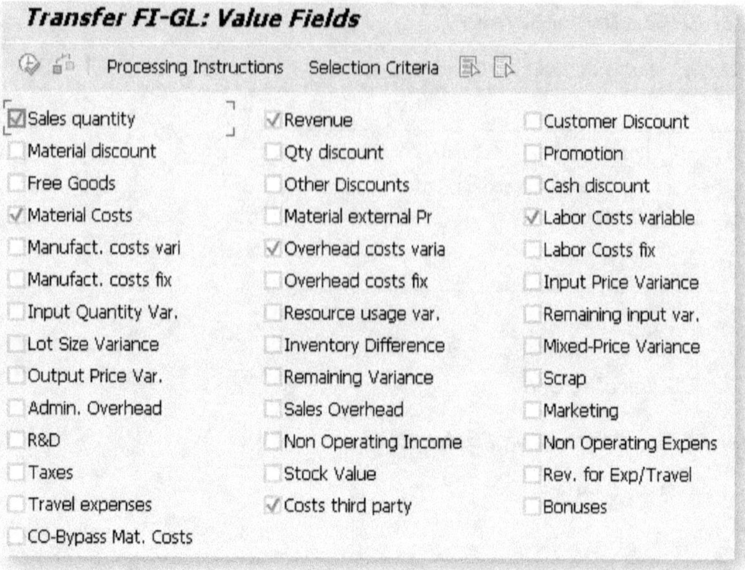

```
Transfer FI-GL: Value Fields

    Processing Instructions   Selection Criteria

☑ Sales quantity          ☑ Revenue                □ Customer Discount
□ Material discount       □ Qty discount           □ Promotion
□ Free Goods              □ Other Discounts        □ Cash discount
☑ Material Costs          □ Material external Pr   ☑ Labor Costs variable
□ Manufact. costs vari    ☑ Overhead costs varia   □ Labor Costs fix
□ Manufact. costs fix     □ Overhead costs fix     □ Input Price Variance
□ Input Quantity Var.     □ Resource usage var.    □ Remaining input var.
□ Lot Size Variance       □ Inventory Difference   □ Mixed-Price Variance
□ Output Price Var.       □ Remaining Variance     □ Scrap
□ Admin. Overhead         □ Sales Overhead         □ Marketing
□ R&D                     □ Non Operating Income   □ Non Operating Expens
□ Taxes                   □ Stock Value            □ Rev. for Exp/Travel
□ Travel expenses         ☑ Costs third party      □ Bonuses
□ CO-Bypass Mat. Costs
```

Figure 4.10: KE1Z select value fields

After executing the transfer, you see planned revenue and cost of goods values in a GL planning version (see Figure 4.11).

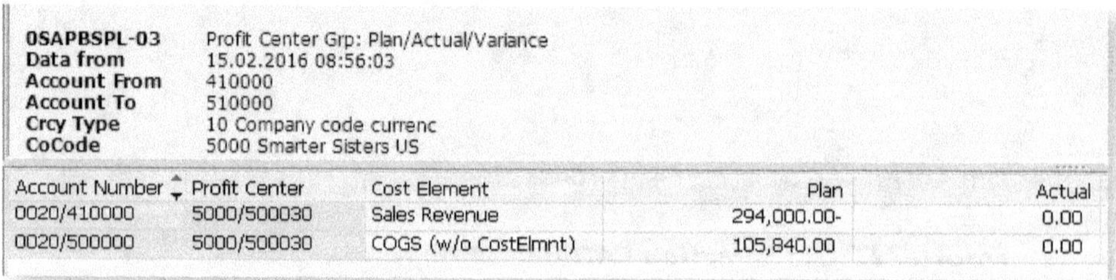

```
0SAPBSPL-03     Profit Center Grp: Plan/Actual/Variance
Data from       15.02.2016 08:56:03
Account From    410000
Account To      510000
Crcy Type       10 Company code currenc
CoCode          5000 Smarter Sisters US
```

Account Number	Profit Center	Cost Element	Plan	Actual
0020/410000	5000/500030	Sales Revenue	294,000.00-	0.00
0020/500000	5000/500030	COGS (w/o CostElmnt)	105,840.00	0.00

Figure 4.11: COPA plan transferred to GL planning

4.4 Integrated cost planning in the new GL

Integrated cost planning in the new GL works similarly to classic PCA. First, as you saw in Figure 4.3, the integrated planning indicator should be set on the planning version. After that, all the CO plan version settings and internal order and project settings for integrated planning seen in Section 3.4 will have the same impact as in classic PCA. As an example, manually enter some cost center plan amounts in KP06 (see Figure 4.12) and see how they flow to plan line items in the new GL with an associated profit center (see Figure 4.13).

Version	1		First Quarter Forecast
Period	1	To	12
Fiscal Year	2016		
Cost Center	5000101900		Production OH - General

Cost Elem...	Plan Fixed Costs	Dis...	Plan Variable Costs	Dis...	Plan fixed cons
540000	560,000.00	2	0.00	2	0.0
581020	240,000.00	2	0.00	2	
581025	110,000.00	2	0.00	2	

Figure 4.12: Cost center planning

Plan Line Items

Year	DocumentNo	Crcy	Ld	R	Ver	Account	Profit Ctr	CoCd	LnItm	Co.cd.curr
2016	12	USD	OL	1	1	540000	500050	5000	000001	560,000.00
2016	12	USD	OL	1	1	581020	500050	5000	000002	240,000.00
2016	12	USD	OL	1	1	581025	500050	5000	000003	110,000.00
*										910,000.00

Figure 4.13: Plan values flow on line to GL

The one major difference between integrated planning in the new GL is in the area of planned allocations. As you are aware, many of the allocation methods in CO use a secondary cost element to move the costs from one cost object to another. The problem is that these secondary cost elements do not exist in the FI chart of accounts. SAP provided a solution to this in the new GL by allowing real-time integration of controlling with financial accounting.

There are a number of steps involved in configuring this, which are beyond the scope of this book and are better dealt with in the context of GL accounting. However, the key piece is the account determination contained in configuration transaction OK17 (see Figure 4.14).

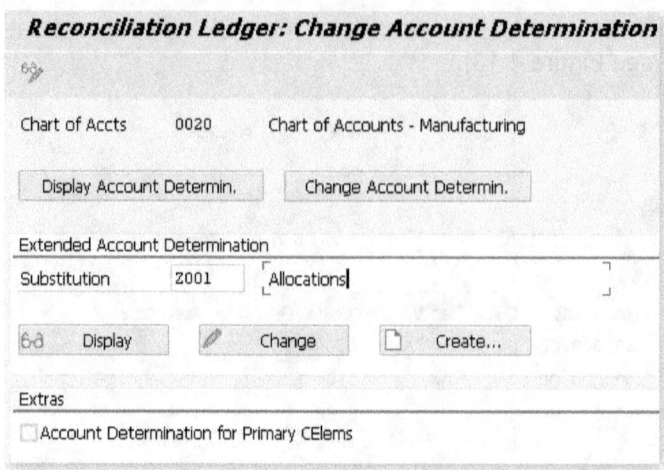

Figure 4.14: FI-CO reconciliation account determination

This account determination will apply for actual postings and for planned values. It is possible to define a combination of a simple account determination using various rules and a more complex account determination using a substitution (see Figure 4.15).

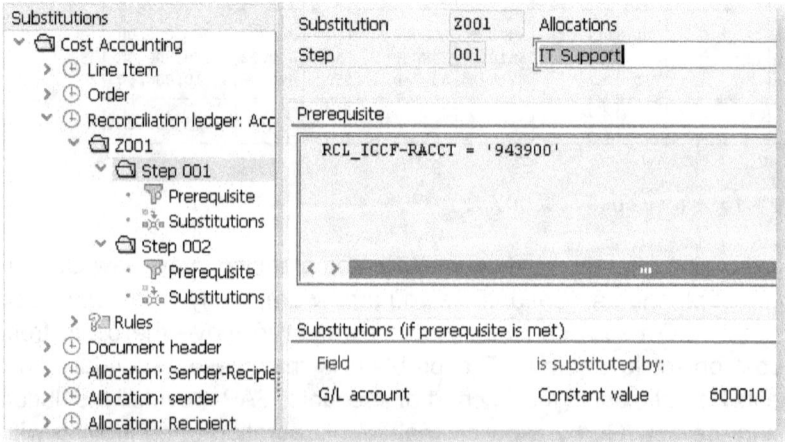

Figure 4.15: Substitution in account determination

In the substitution, you can build the rules needed to determine the account mapping. Make a simple replacement of a secondary cost element with a constant-value GL account.

Depending on your system configuration it may also be necessary to activate plan integration for secondary cost elements using configuration transaction FAGL_PLAN_ACT_SEC. This is normally deactivated by default in an SAP system (see Figure 4.16). Once you execute this, the plan integration becomes active (see Figure 4.17).

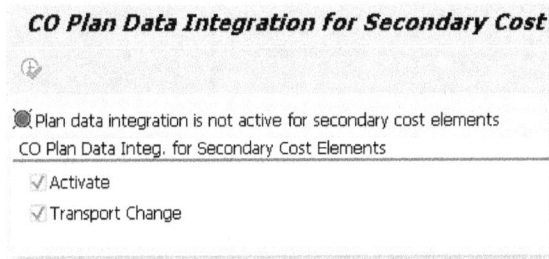

Figure 4.16: Inactive plan integration of secondary cost element

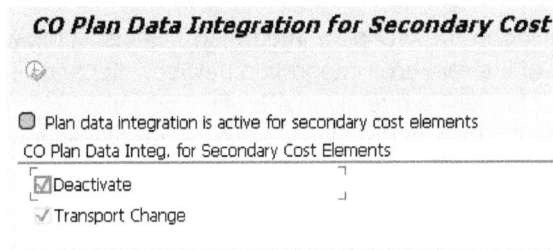

Figure 4.17: Active plan integration of secondary cost elements

When performing an activity allocation to plan consumption of IT support activities in a customer cost center in the standard cost center planning transaction KP06 (see Figure 4.18), you should see an online transfer into the new GL plan using the account that you defined in your substitution rule (see Figure 4.19).

Version	1			First Quarter Forecast					
Period	1		To	12					
Fiscal Year	2016								
Cost Center	5000101900			Production OH - General					
Sender Co...	Send...	Plan fixed consu...	Dis...	Plan vbl consum...	Dis...	U...	Plan fixed costs	Plan Variable Costs	Alloc. cost
500010210	50010	600	2	0	2	H	24,000.00	0.00	943900

Figure 4.18: Cost center activity input planning

97

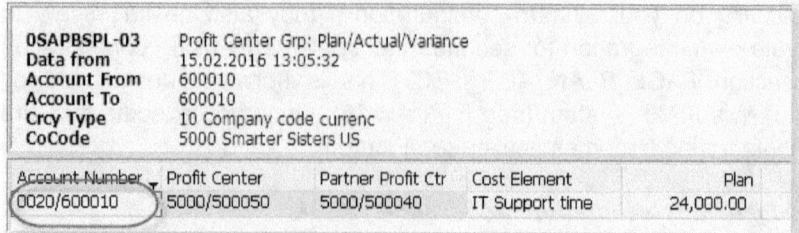

Figure 4.19: Activity input plan flows to GL

The same is true for plan assessments, overhead calculations, and settlements.

4.5 Statistical key figure planning in the GL

Statistical key figure planning in the CO plan integrated objects will flow into GL planning because of the real-time integration between CO and FI. It is also possible to post plan SKFs directly in GL planning using transaction FAGLSKF1, however, these plan values will only be available in the GL and not in CO.

4.6 Manual planning in the new GL

Manual planning in the new GL may be required for exactly the same reasons as manual planning in classic PCA. That is balance sheet items, costs and revenues not transferred from COPA; or cost objects, planned assessments, and distributions within the GL; and manual SKF planning.

Manual planning in the new GL requires planning layouts and planner profiles similar to planning in CO. There is a delivered planner profile called SAPFAGL for new GL planning with some layouts already assigned to it. If you require custom layouts, you can copy that standard planner profile and use the copy to contain any new layouts that you create.

There are a few different steps involved in setting up layouts and profiles for GL planning. To create the layouts, it is necessary to go through the SAP IMG following the menu path SAP CUSTOMIZING IMPLEMENTATION GUIDE • FINANCIAL ACCOUNTING (NEW) • GENERAL LEDGER ACCOUNTING (NEW) • PLANNING • DEFINE PLANNING LAYOUT. Select the option to create planning layout and then select summary tables (see Figure 4.20). Unless you are using public sector accounting, you should select FAGLFLEXT.

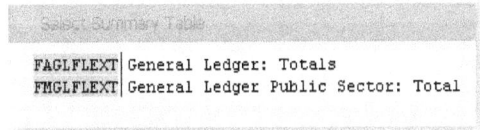

Figure 4.20: Select summary tables for planning layout

Next is the initial screen for creating the layout (Figure 4.21) where you enter a layout name and description. You also can copy an existing layout, if required.

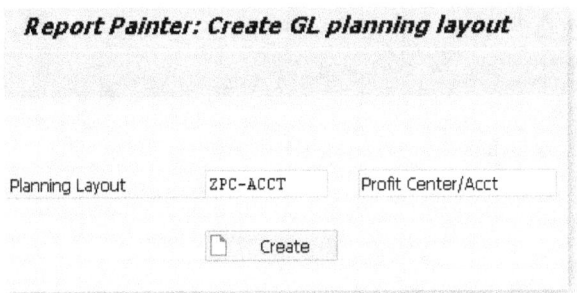

Figure 4.21: Create GL planning layout

> **Termination error**
>
> If you get an unexpected termination error (short dump) when displaying or maintaining the planning layouts or you get an error trying to create a planner profile with FAGLFLEXT, you may need to run transaction GLPLINSTALL first to install the planning summary tables.

Again, you want to have a planning layout that allows you to enter plan values for the combination of profit center and account on a monthly basis. Just as you did for classic PCA, you can build this using the report painter functionality (see Figure 4.22). Again, all the characteristics required for planning must be included somewhere in the layout.

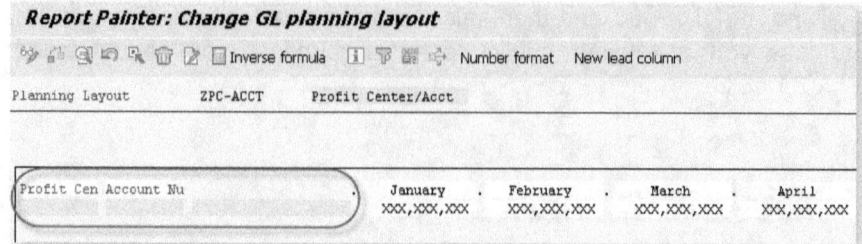

Figure 4.22: Building a GL planning layout

Once you have the layout, assign it to the planner profile using the configuration transaction GLPLADM. I created a copy of the SAP delivered profile and named it ZSAPFAGL (see Figure 4.23).

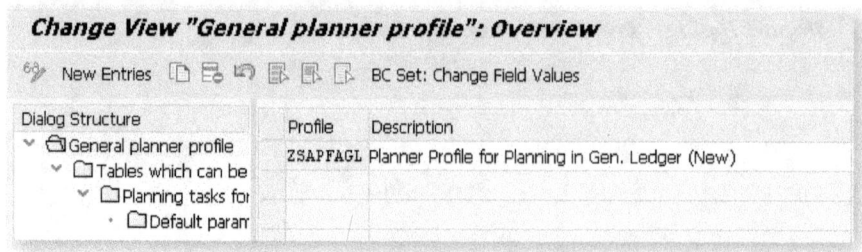

Figure 4.23: Planner profile general screen

Now you see a level for the totals TABLES WHICH CAN BE PLANNED. If you copied the SAP delivered profile, you should only see the FAGLFLEXT table (see Figure 4.24). That is the correct totals table for new GL planning. You can assign default distribution keys for both the currency values and quantity values used in manual planning in the new GL.

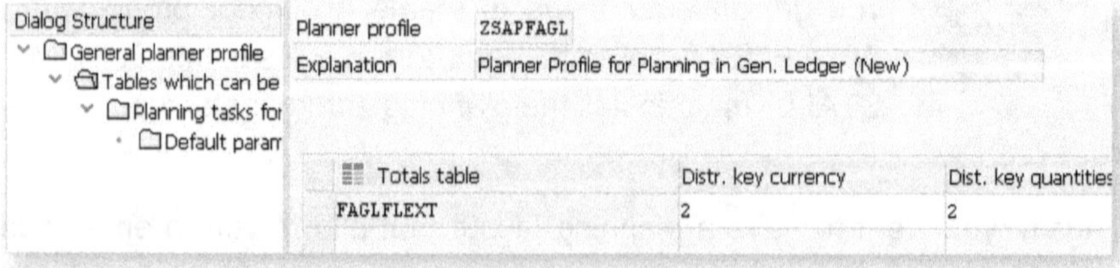

Figure 4.24: Totals tables to be planned

The next level down is the PLANNING TASKS FOR THE TABLE. It is at this level that you assign your planning layout (see Figure 4.25). You have an integrated Excel check box here to open the planning in Excel and to also create an Excel template for upload. You can also assign your planning document type and the exchange rate for manual planning.

Planner profile	ZSAPFAGL									
Summary table	FAGLFLEXT									
Explanation	Planner Profile for Planning in Gen. Ledger (New)									
It...	Layout	Text for Plan Task	De...	C...	Sum...	Int...	Docu...	Exch.....	Tr...	Cu...
50	ZPC-ACCT	Profit Center/Account		✓	✓	PO	M	✓		
100	0FAGL-01	Profitcenter, Konto		✓		PO	M	✓		
110	0FAGL-02	Profitcenter-Gruppe, Konto		✓		PO	M	✓		
120	0FAGL-03	Segment, Konto		✓		PO	M	✓		
130	0FAGL-04	ProfitCtr, FunktBereich, Konto		✓		PO	M	✓		
140	0FAGL-05	Partner-PrCtr, PrCtr, Konto		✓		PO	M	✓		
150	0FAGL-06	Kostenstelle, Konto		✓		PO	M	✓		
160	0FAGL-07	Konto		✓		PO	M	✓		

Figure 4.25: Assign the layout

The next folder down is for entering the DEFAULT PARAMETERS for the planning layout (see Figure 4.26). You need to go here if you want to create a template for uploading your plan.

Plan data Change Default Parameters

Tab layout

Layout	ZPC-ACCT	Profit Center/Acct
Variables		
Company Code	5000	Smarter Sisters US
Ledger	0L	IFRS Ledger
Version	1	First Quarter Forecast
Fiscal Year	2016	
Transaction currency	USD	United States Dollar
Account Number	131000	Inventory - Raw Material
to	135075	Inventory - Trading Goods

Figure 4.26: Default parameters for GL manual planning

Click the OVERVIEW button to open the layout in an Excel format. You will receive a message about the file description being generated and then you see the layout in Excel (see Figure 4.27). You may have to accept macros or otherwise change some security settings in Excel if it does not work immediately.

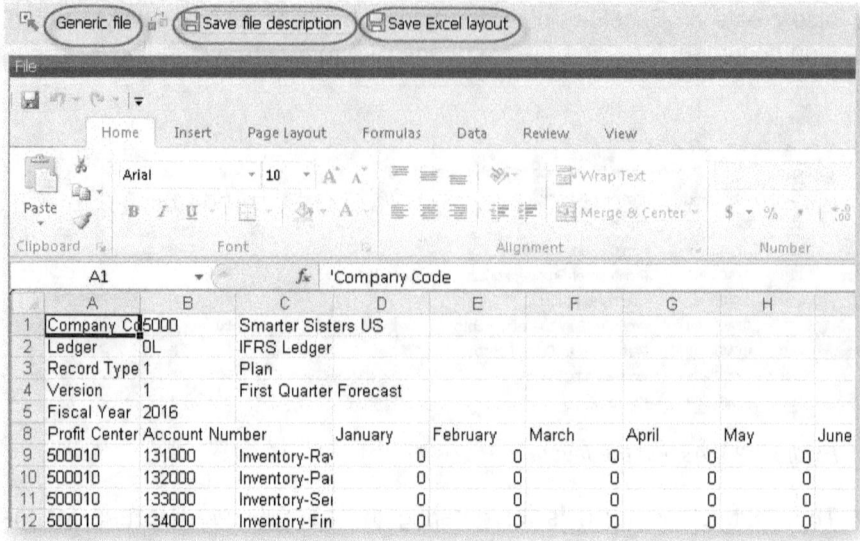

Figure 4.27: GL planning in an Excel layout

The rest of the steps are identical to what you did in Section 3.6 to generate the generic file and the file description.

Once you are finished, you should see the file description assigned to your planning layout (see Figure 4.28).

Figure 4.28: File description assigned to planning layout

Once you have a layout and a planner profile, you can enter planning directly in SAP or through an upload using your saved template. In the new GL, the transaction for uploading is GLPLUP – Upload from Excel. It looks the same as the upload you used in classic PCA and works in the same manner (see Figure 4.29).

Again, the key is to make sure that the file description matches what is assigned to your layout. When you execute, you will get a message telling if you were successful or not (see Figure 4.30) and you should see the planned data in the GL (see Figure 4.31).

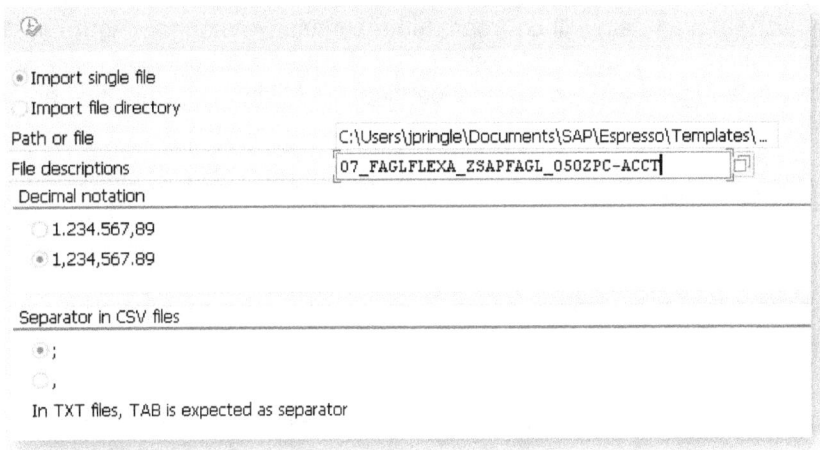

Figure 4.29: Upload plan to GL planning

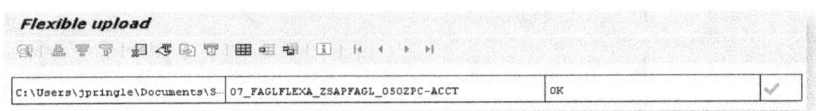

Figure 4.30: GL plan upload message

OSAPBSPL-03	Profit Center Grp: Plan/Actual/Variance
Data from	17.02.2016 10:45:18
Account From	131000
Account To	136000
Crcy Type	10 Company code currenc
CoCode	5000 Smarter Sisters US
CO Area	5000 Smarter Sisters

Account Number	Profit Center	Plan
0020/131000	5000/500010	130,000.00
0020/132000	5000/500010	45,000.00
0020/134000	5000/500010	60,000.00

Figure 4.31: Plan uploaded in GL with profit center

You saw in Section 3.6 how classic PCA planning treats balance sheet plan postings as cumulative values and only posts changes as line items. In the new GL, you actually have two options. By default, the system will not treat GL balance sheet plans in a cumulative manner so you should load the plan as an opening balance and periodic changes. If you want the GL balance sheet plan to behave in the same way as classic PCA, then you must make a configuration change in the SAP IMG. Do this

103

under FINANCIAL ACCOUNTING (NEW) • GENERAL LEDGER ACCOUNTING (NEW) • PLANNING • ACTIVATE CUMULATIVE PLAN DATA ENTRY FOR BALANCE SHEET ACCOUNTS (see Figure 4.32). Check the box and save. The balance sheet plan data will be treated in a cumulative manner. Figure 4.31 shows plan data loaded for periods 1 to 4 with the cumulative entry active, while Figure 4.33 shows the identical load with the cumulative entry inactive.

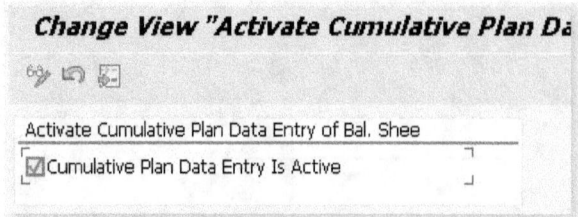

Figure 4.32: Activate cumulative balance sheet planning

```
0SAPBSPL-03      Profit Center Grp: Plan/Actual/Variance
Data from        17.02.2016 11:05:14
Account From     131000
Account To       136000
Crcy Type        10 Company code currenc
CoCode           5000 Smarter Sisters US
```

Account Number	Profit Center	Plan
0020/131000	5000/500010	520,000.00
0020/132000	5000/500010	180,000.00
0020/134000	5000/500010	240,000.00

Figure 4.33: Plan without cumulative entry

As with classic PCA, you can carry forward plan values into the following year using transaction FAGL_PLAN_VT. The balance carry forward option only works if you have activated the cumulative balance sheet planning.

Direct manual planning is done using transaction GP12N and any layout associated with your planner profile (see Figure 4.34). This is no different to the direct manual planning that you saw in classic PCA. The selection criteria and the values on the planning screens are controlled by the planning layout that you are using. If there are multiple planning layouts linked to your planner profile, you can toggle through them using the FORWARD and BACK buttons.

PROFIT CENTER PLANNING IN THE NEW GL

```
       Tab layout    Profile
Layout              OFAGL-01     Profit Ctr, Account
Variables
  From Period       1                        January
  To Period         12                       December
  Profit Center     500040                   US Corporate
  Company Code      5000                     Smarter Sisters US
  Ledger            0L                       IFRS Ledger
  Version           1                        First Quarter Forecast
  Fiscal Year       2016
  Currency          USD                      United States Dollar
  Account Number    701000                   Extraordinary Expenses / Income
         to         701000                   Extraordinary Expenses / Income
```

Figure 4.34: Manual GL planning initial screen

Next, go into the planning screen (see Figure 4.35) by pressing the OVERVIEW button, or alternatively, pressing the PERIOD SCREEN button to plan at an individual period level. Manually plan some expenses that are beyond the control of an individual cost center and that won't be transferred online. You have the same functionality as in PCA with distribution keys and the ability to edit at the period level. After posting, the item is visible in any of the GL reports supporting a plan view (see Figure 4.36).

```
Plan data Change Cumulative Vals

  Posting period   1                To    12
  Profit Center    500040                 US Corporate
  Company Code     5000                   Smarter Sisters US
  Ledger           0L                     IFRS Ledger
  Record Type      1                      Plan
  Version          1                      First Quarter Forecast
  Fiscal Year      2016
  Currency         USD                    United States Dollar

  Account N... Text              Trans. Currency      Dis... Unit
    701000   Extraord Exp/Inc         240,000.00    7     USD
```

Figure 4.35: Enter manual plan values

105

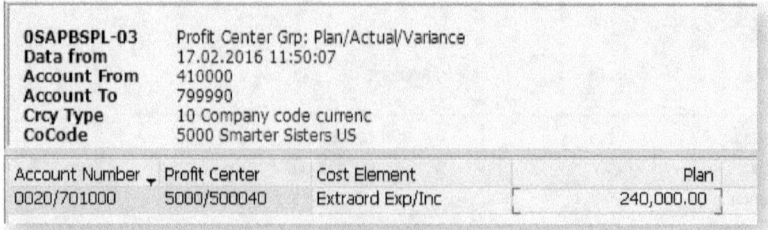

Figure 4.36: Manual item posted to GL plan

Manual planning in the new GL also allows you to create planned assessments and distributions. These are similar to what was discussed for classic PCA. They can be executed using FAGLGA2B for assessment and FAGLGA4B for distribution. The major difference is in the setup of the assessment cycle. Since you cannot use a secondary cost element in the GL, you have to define a GL account to take that role.

Finally, GL manual planning also gives you a tool for copying data into plans—similar to what you saw in classic PCA. In the GL, this transaction is FAGLGP52 (see Figure 4.37).

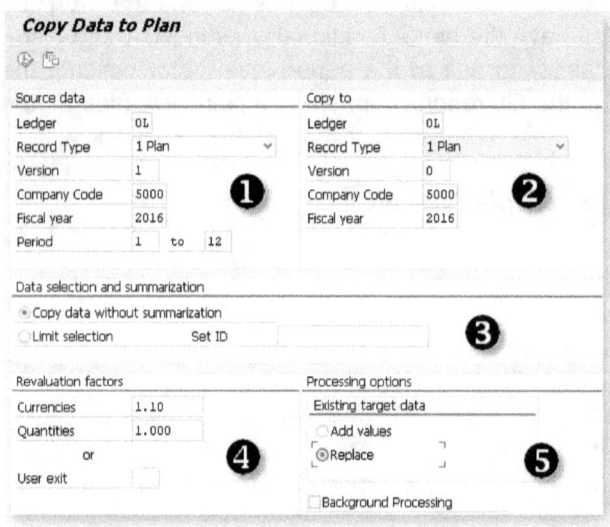

Figure 4.37: GL copy data to plan

On the initial screen, there are a number of sections to define the copy parameters. ❶ The SOURCE DATA—where you can select the RECORD TYPE as actual, plan, actual assessment/distribution, planned assessment distribution, or year-end closing posting. Here you also select the ledger, version, company code, and fiscal year to copy from. ❷ In the COPY TO section, you define the ledger, version, company code, and fiscal year to receive the copy. ❸ In the DATA SELECTION AND SUMMARIZATION section, you can decide to copy the data as is or apply a summarization based on a defined set. This is useful if the copy-from data contains dimensions that you do not want to include in your copy. For example, if you are planning the dimensions account and profit center but the copy-from data also includes cost center, you can build a set containing only the dimensions that you require and copy the plan based on that level of summarization. ❹ You can apply a REVALUATION FACTOR to the plan data being copied, such as increase the plan by 10%. For complex plan revaluation, you can define a *user exit* and link it. ❺ Finally, you can decide what happens with EXISTING PLAN DATA—whether it will be added to or overwritten.

After executing the copy, you see the copied amounts increased by 10% in the target version (see Figure 4.38).

0SAPBSPL-04	Profit Center Group: Plan/Plan/Actual				
Data from	17.02.2016 12:54:16				
Crcy Type	10 Company code currenc				
CoCode	5000 Smarter Sisters US				
CO Area	5000 Smarter Sisters				
Profit Center	50001 US Region				

Account Number	Profit Center	Cost Element		Plan OL/1	Plan OL/0
0020/540000	5000/500050	Salaries		560,000.00	616,000.04
0020/540000	5000/500040	Salaries		600,000.00	660,000.00
0020/581020	5000/500050	Communications		240,000.00	264,000.00
0020/581025	5000/500050	Computer S/Hardware		110,000.00	121,000.04
0020/582010	5000/500010	Marketing & Promotio		480,000.00	528,000.00
0020/600010	5000/500040	IT Support time		352,000.00-	387,200.00-
0020/701000	5000/500040	Extraord Exp/Inc		240,000.00	264,000.01

Figure 4.38: Result of plan copy

In the past two chapters, you looked at the planning functions in both classic PCA and the new GL. You saw plan integration and manual planning tools. Now, with your planning data in place, it is time to see how to get actual results for comparisons.

4.7 Summary

In this chapter, you learned how planning works for profit center accounting in the new GL. You saw how the new GL planning fits into an overall planning cycle that can include COPA planning, cost center and cost object planning, and sales and operations planning. You saw the planning version concept in the new GL and how the setup of versions differs between new GL planning and CO. You learned about integrated revenue planning and integrated cost planning with the new GL and you saw which settings allow plan data to flow from other SAP objects into new GL planning. You looked at statistical key figures planning in the new GL and how it can be integrated with SKF planning in controlling. You learned about manual planning in new GL planning. You learned about planning layouts and planner profiles and how to use techniques such as flexible Excel upload and plan copy functionality. In the next chapter, you will start to see how both classic PCA and the new GL PCA fit within the flow of actual transactions in SAP.

5 Profit center actual postings

In this chapter, I explain the flow of actual values from other SAP ECC modules into PCA. I address the concept of document splitting and the scenario concept in the new GL and show the period-end processes within PCA and explain the differences between classic PCA and new GL PCA.

5.1 Flow of actual values in classic PCA

Actual values flow into PCA either periodically or in real time from a variety of sources (see Figure 5.1).

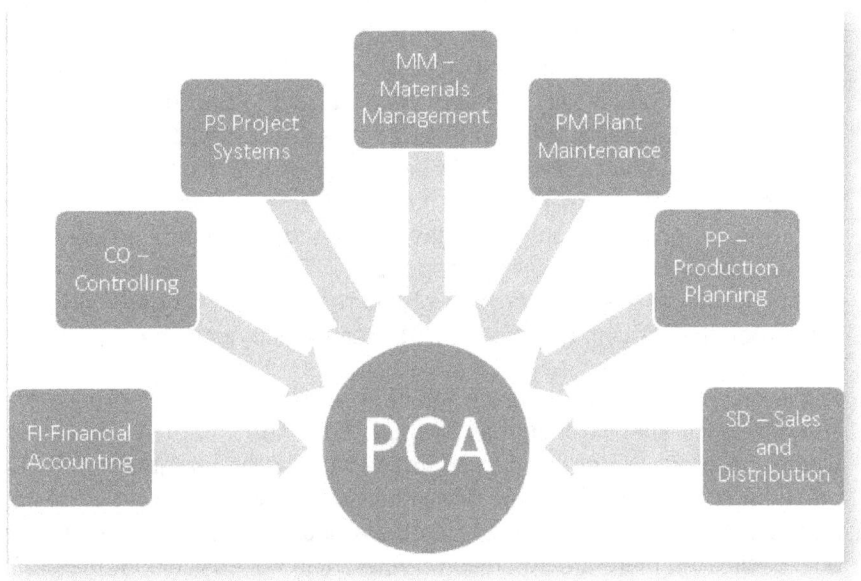

Figure 5.1: Value flow into classic PCA

Most of this data can be set to transfer online directly into PCA. The key piece of configuration relating to the flow of actual values into classic PCA is the control parameters for actual postings, transaction 1KEF (see Figure 5.2). You can set the system to transfer line items and define whether you want to transfer data online or by using the periodic programs. It is generally recommended to use both line items and online transfer. You can also lock the combination of CONTROLLING AREA and FROM YEAR against actual postings.

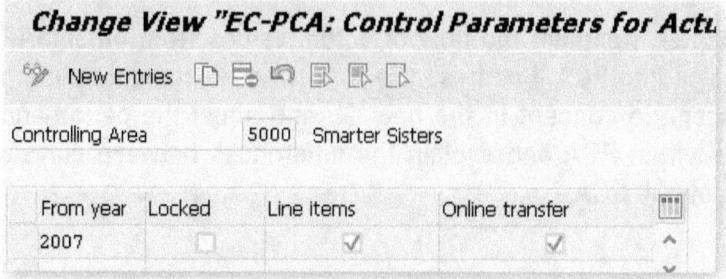

Figure 5.2: Control parameters for actual posting

When thinking about the flow of actual values into classic PCA, it is useful to differentiate between P&L values and balance sheet values. For the most part, P&L accounts have a cost or revenue element associated with them. This means that postings to these accounts require an attached CO object. This object may be a cost center, internal order, WBS element, or COPA profitability segment. You learned in Section 2.8 that other than the profitability segment, all of these CO objects should have profit centers manually assigned to them. Due to this, most cost postings receive the profit center based on that assignment. Cost of goods sold and revenue postings come from the sales and distribution transactions of *post goods issue* and *billing* respectively. They get their profit center assignment from the sales order. For this reason, there is generally very little problem in getting a complete P&L statement by profit center.

In the classic PCA, the balance sheet is a bit more difficult. There are some balance sheet values that flow directly online into PCA. These are where the profit center can be determined based on assignment. There are others, such as payables and receivables, where the profit center must be determined retroactively, so they must be transferred on a periodic basis. And there are some items where it is not possible for the profit center to be determined, so you must enter the transaction manually if you want the value to be posted in PCA (see Figure 5.3).

For inventory, WIP, and fixed assets it is possible to have online transfers, but there are also periodic transfer options available. For payables and receivables, you can only perform the transfer on a periodic basis. All other balance sheet items require manual intervention.

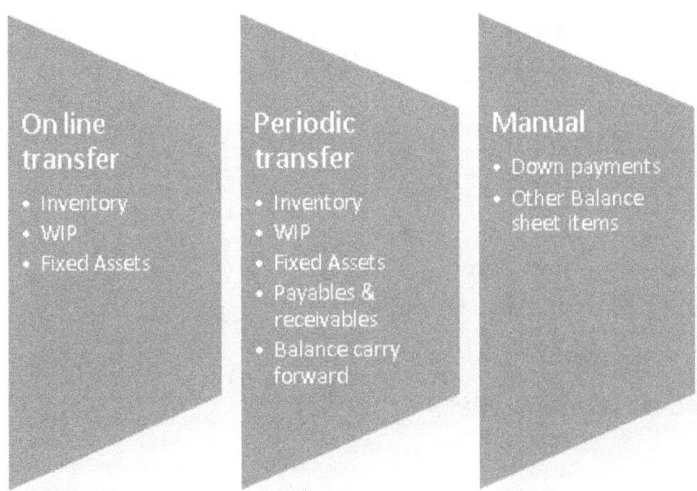

Figure 5.3: Transfer of balance sheet items

In addition to the control parameters (shown in Figure 5.2), you also need to define the balance sheet and P&L accounts to transfer to PCA in transaction 3KEH. Here, you define the accounts and a default profit center associated with each account or range of accounts (see Figure 5.4). Then you can also branch to a more detailed profit center derivation by clicking on the PrCtr Det button. This takes you directly to transaction KED0 where you can build detailed derivation rules for profit center determination (see Figure 5.5). By clicking on the button, you go to a screen to set up rule values based on defined source fields (see Figure 5.6). You can derive the profit center for ranges of accounts based on company code and valuation area (plant). Note that you cannot define ranges of accounts in the rule that are different from the ranges you defined in 3KEH.

Payables and receivables in 3KEH

 You should not define your payables and receivables reconciliation accounts in 3KEH since these are transferred using a process that actually reads the items in the sub-ledgers.

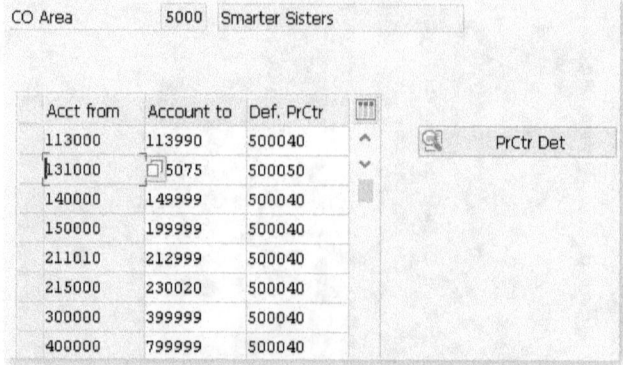

Figure 5.4: Accounts to transfer to PCA

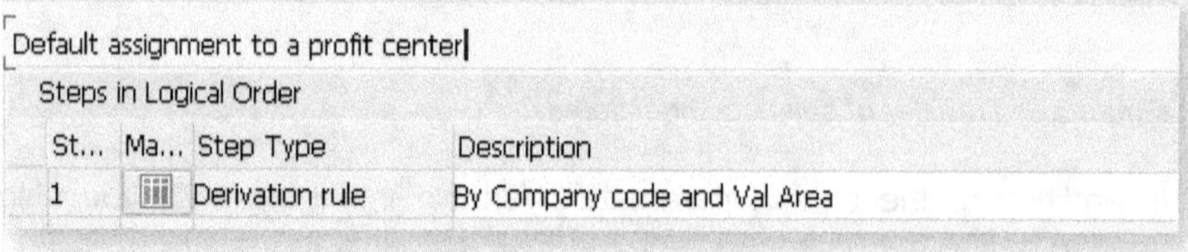

Figure 5.5: Initial screen for profit center derivation

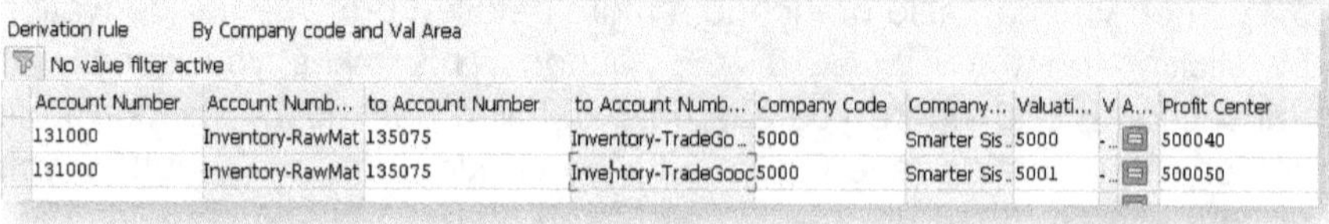

Figure 5.6: Derivation rule for profit center

Once you set up the configuration for online posting and for the additional accounts, run the manual transfer programs to post any existing balances.

> **Manual transfer for online items**
>
>  When you run the manual transfer, any existing data that has already been transferred is overwritten. This is important to note since online postings usually contain a level of detail based on individually posted documents while a manual transfer creates summarized postings based on an object. If you run a manual transfer after having online postings, you lose that level of detail in PCA.

The periodic transfer transactions are:

- 1KEH for inventory
- 1KEJ for work in process (WIP)
- 1KEI for fixed assets
- 1KEK for payables and receivables

The basic functionality and look of these transactions is very similar, so only the payables and receivables process details will be explained. First, take a look at the value flow for the three online processes.

For any transactions relating to inventory, the profit center is derived from the plant-specific material master information. All material movements are carried out using a plant and material master. For example, you may want to move some inventory from the manufacturing plant to a distribution center (see Figure 5.7). You see that this transfer makes a profit center posting as the plant-specific data on this material belongs to two different profit centers (see Figure 5.8).

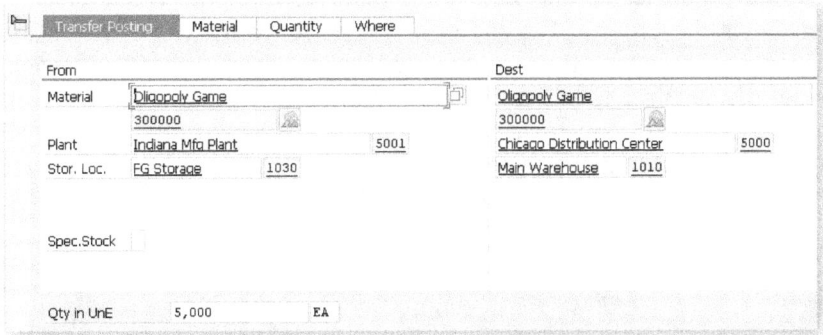

Figure 5.7: Material transfer between plants

Ledger	8A
Controlling Area	5000
Company Code	5000
Posting Period	002
Fiscal Year	2016
Version	000

D	Ref.Doc.No.	Itm	Period	Profit Center	Partner PC	Account	Acc.Text	Σ In pctr local curr.	Curr.	Quantity
W	4900000062	1	2	500050	500020	134000	Inventory-FinGoods	28,950.00-	USD	5,000-
W	4900000062	2	2	500020	500050	134000	Inventory-FinGoods	28,950.00	USD	5,000
								• **0.00**	**USD**	

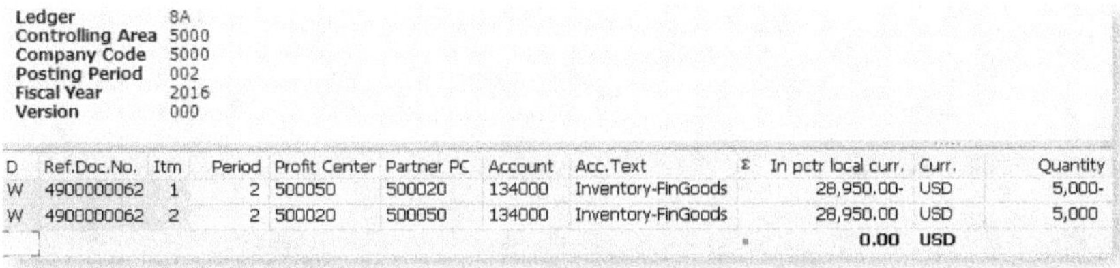

Figure 5.8: Profit center posting for material transfer

In SAP, WIP calculation is a type of result analysis that makes a financial posting at period end to move any balances for incomplete production orders from the P&L to the balance sheet for overall reporting purposes.

It is strictly a financial posting with no controlling impact, however, the WIP posting picks up a profit center assignment from the plant and material combination of the production order.

For example, consider a production order to produce 5,000 games for which you have only completed 1,000 (see Figure 5.9).

Order	1000004					Type	YBM1
Material	300000		Oligopoly Game			Plant	5001
Status	REL PCNF PRC GMPS MACM PDLV SETC						

General	Assignment	Goods Receipt	Control	Dates/Qties	Master Data	Long Text

Quantities						
Total Qty	5,000	EA	Scrap Portion	0	0.00	%
Delivered	1,000		Short/Exc. Rcpt	0		

Figure 5.9: Production order partial delivery

You have actually issued materials and activities to this order which remain as a balance in the order costs (see Figure 5.10). If this balance remains in the order at the end of a period, you want it to show on the balance sheet rather than on the P&L, where it is currently showing, since it is technically still an asset and not a cost. If you run the WIP transaction, KKAX and settle the order using KO88, you see that the WIP posting picks up the profit center (see Figure 5.11) and your balance sheet receives a debit and the P&L a credit.

Order	1000006 000000000000300000
Order Type	YBM1 MTS Production Order
Plant	5001 Indiana Mfg Plant
Material	300000 Oligopoly Game

Planned Quantity	5,000 EA each
Actual Quantity	1,000 EA each

Cost Elem.	Cost Element (Text)	Origin	Σ	Total act.costs	Currency
510020	Consumption - Finished Goods	5001/300000		5,790.00-	USD
510000	Consumption - Raw Materials			0.00	USD
510000	Consumption - Raw Materials	5001/100070		0.00	USD
510000	Consumption - Raw Materials	5001/100071		0.00	USD
510000	Consumption - Raw Materials	5001/100073		0.00	USD
943000	Production Labour	5000101199/1000		750.00	USD
943010	Production Overhead	5000101199/1100		1,375.00	USD
			*	7,331.95	USD
			**	7,331.95	USD

Figure 5.10: Balance of costs in a production order

PROFIT CENTER ACTUAL POSTINGS

Ledger		8A							
Controlling Area		5000							
Company Code		5000							
Posting Period		002							
Fiscal Year		2016							
Version		000							

D	Ref.	Itm	Period	Profit Center	Account	Acc.Text	Σ	In pctr local curr.	Curr.
W	5	1	2	500050	539999	WIP Offset		7,331.95-	USD
W	5	2	2	500050	136000	Inventory-WIP		7,331.95	USD
								0.00	USD

Figure 5.11: WIP posting online to PCA

For fixed assets, the profit center is determined from the cost center assigned on the asset master. This flows through into any balance sheet posting involving that asset. For example, if you post a standard acquisition using transaction ABZON (see Figure 5.12), you get a posting to PCA to the derived profit center (see Figure 5.13).

Company Code	5000		Smarter Sisters US
● Existing asset	20006	0	Fork Lift truck for plant
○ New asset			MasterData
	Description		
	Asset Class		
	Cost Center		

Transaction data	Additional Details	Note

Area Selection

Ledger Group	
Depreciation Area	

Basic Data

Document Date	19.02.2016	
Posting Date	19.02.2016	
Asset Value Date	19.02.2016	
Amount posted	35,000.00	USD
Quantity	1.000	EA

Figure 5.12: Enter asset acquisition

PROFIT CENTER ACTUAL POSTINGS

```
Ledger              8A
Controlling Area    5000
Company Code        5000
Posting Period      002
Fiscal Year         2016
Version             000
```

D	Ref.D	Itm	Period	Profit Center	Account	Acc.Text	Σ In pctr local curr.	Curr.
W	1	1	2	500050	160040	F/A-Mobile Equip	35,000.00	USD
W	1	2	2	500050	217200	Other Liabilities	35,000.00-	USD
							0.00	USD

Figure 5.13: Asset posting in PCA

The process for payables and receivables is slightly different since it cannot happen online. In addition, you want the payable or receivable to post to the correct profit center in line with the individual line items of the invoice or billing document. For example, you may have accounts payables (AP) invoices where the expense items are split between multiple profit centers, as shown in Figure 5.14. You want the AP amount to transfer into PCA in the same proportion as the expense.

Data Entry View

Document Number	1900000001	Company Code	5000	Fiscal Year	2016
Document Date	19.02.2016	Posting Date	19.02.2016	Period	2
Reference	86868796	Cross-Comp.No.			
Currency	USD	Texts exist		Ledger Group	

Co	Itm	PK	Account	Description	Amount	Curr.	Cost Center	Profit Ctr
5000	1	31	100026	Countem Wright Auditors	17,000.00-	USD		
5000	2	40	581705	Audit fees	10,000.00	USD	5000102001	500040
5000	3	40	581705	Audit fees	7,000.00	USD	5000101900	500050

Figure 5.14: AP invoice two profit centers

For this to happen, you need to run transaction F.5D to calculate a balance sheet adjustment (see Figure 5.15). This actually performs a document splitting on the AP or accounts receivables (AR) document. You simply enter or choose your `company code(s)` and click the ⊕ button.

Calculate Balance Sheet Adjustment

Company code	5000	to	

Figure 5.15: Calculate AP and AR split

You get a message that the system has calculated a breakdown for some documents. If you want to see what has actually happened, you can go back to display the original financial document in FB03. From the ENVIRONMENT menu, select BALANCE SHEET ADJUSTMENT (see Figure 5.16). Here, you can see that the adjustment program has split the vendor item between the two profit centers in the same proportion as the expense items.

```
Document number    1900000001
Company code       5000
Fiscal Year        2016
```

Itm	PK	Account	BA	TPBA	Profit ctr	TP ProfCtr	Amount in USD
001	31	100026					17,000.00-
					500040		10,000.00-
					500050		7,000.00-
002	40	581705			500040		10,000.00
003	40	581705			500050		7,000.00

Figure 5.16: Display balance sheet adjustment for AP invoice

After the balance sheet adjustment has been done, use 1KEK (Figure 5.17) to transfer the payables and receivables to PCA.

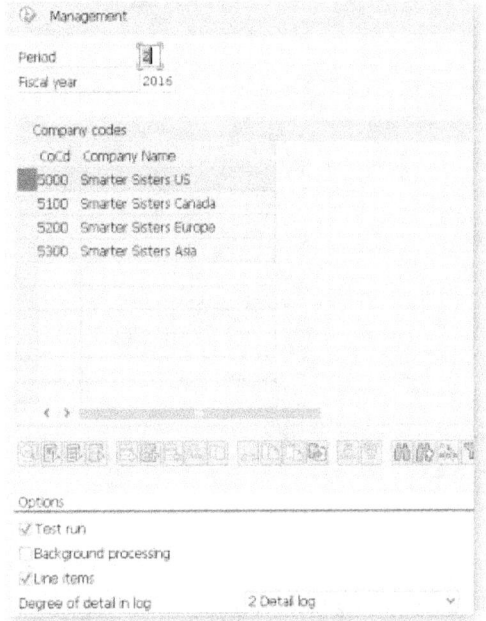

Figure 5.17: Transfer payables and receivables

You need to select the `period` and the `fiscal year` for the transfer and then choose one or more company codes. You then have options for `test run, background processing, line items,` and `detail log`. Clicking the 👉 button without `test run` selected will post the data to PCA (Figure 5.18).

> **Run in test mode**
>
>
> Many SAP periodic processing transactions provide a test mode option. It is recommended to use it to see potential errors or to expose inconsistencies in postings before finally committing the posting. In the case of 1KEK, it is useful to run in test mode with line items and a detailed log to see the profit center distribution in advance. If anything is going to the dummy profit center, you may be able to correct it before posting

EC-PCA: Transfer payables and receivables

Company code: 5000 Smarter Sisters US
Period: 02
Fiscal year: 2016

Update Run w. Line Items

G/L Acc	Customer	Vendor	Profit Center Σ	Amount	Crcy
121000	100016		500020	1,495.00	USD
121000				1,495.00	USD
211000		100026	500040	10,000.00-	USD
		100025	500050	12,000.00-	USD
		100026	500050	7,000.00-	USD
		100027	500050	18,750.00-	USD
		100028	500050	5,000.00-	USD
		100029	500050	88,000.00-	USD
		100030	500050	10,687.02-	USD
		100031	500050	34,751.77-	USD
		100032	500050	35,000.00-	USD
		100033	500050	10,000.00-	USD
211000				231,188.79-	USD
				229,693.79-	USD

Figure 5.18: Detail log of running 1KEK

The vendor balances and items can be displayed in PCA in the report S_ALR_87013344 – Profit Center: Payables (see Figure 5.19).

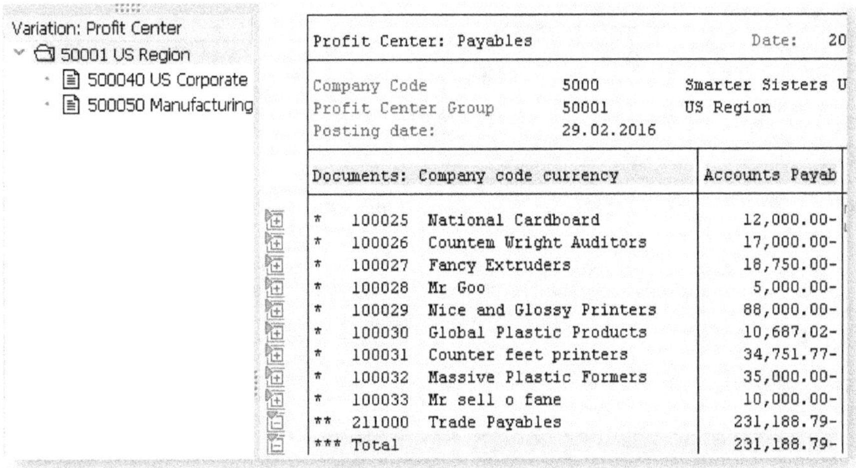

PROFIT CENTER ACTUAL POSTINGS

```
Variation: Profit Center
 ⌵ 🗁 50001 US Region
    · 📄 500040 US Corporate
    · 📄 500050 Manufacturing
```

Profit Center: Payables		Date: 20
Company Code	5000	Smarter Sisters U
Profit Center Group	50001	US Region
Posting date:	29.02.2016	

Documents: Company code currency			Accounts Payab
*	100025	National Cardboard	12,000.00-
*	100026	Countem Wright Auditors	17,000.00-
*	100027	Fancy Extruders	18,750.00-
*	100028	Mr Goo	5,000.00-
*	100029	Nice and Glossy Printers	88,000.00-
*	100030	Global Plastic Products	10,687.02-
*	100031	Counter feet printers	34,751.77-
*	100032	Massive Plastic Formers	35,000.00-
*	100033	Mr sell o fane	10,000.00-
**	211000	Trade Payables	231,188.79-
***		Total	231,188.79-

Figure 5.19: Vendor balances and open items in PCA

From a payables and receivables standpoint there may be some subsequent P&L postings related to the payment of these items, such as realized foreign exchange gain or loss, and cash discounts given or received based on terms of payment. As an example, consider an invoice for marketing materials that has been entered to three different profit centers in Canadian dollars (see Figure 5.20).

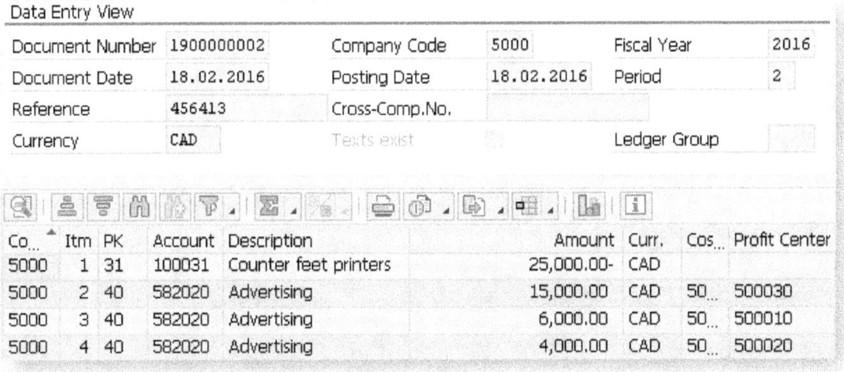

Data Entry View					
Document Number	1900000002	Company Code	5000	Fiscal Year	2016
Document Date	18.02.2016	Posting Date	18.02.2016	Period	2
Reference	456413	Cross-Comp.No.			
Currency	CAD	Texts exist		Ledger Group	

Co...	Itm	PK	Account	Description	Amount	Curr.	Cos...	Profit Center
5000	1	31	100031	Counter feet printers	25,000.00-	CAD		
5000	2	40	582020	Advertising	15,000.00	CAD	50...	500030
5000	3	40	582020	Advertising	6,000.00	CAD	50...	500010
5000	4	40	582020	Advertising	4,000.00	CAD	50...	500020

Figure 5.20: Foreign currency invoice

Between the time the invoice is posted and the time the vendor is paid, the exchange rate has changed between CAD and USD, giving rise to a realized exchange gain on the payment (see Figure 5.21).

119

Data Entry View

Document Number	1500000002	Company Code	5000		Fiscal Year		2016
Document Date	20.02.2016	Posting Date	20.02.2016		Period		2
Reference		Cross-Comp.No.					
Currency	CAD	Texts exist			Ledger Group		

Co...	Itm	PK	Account	Description	Amount	Curr.	Cost Center	Profit Ctr
5000	1	50	113005	CIBC C$-Checks Out	17,421.60-	USD		
5000	2	25	100031	Counter feet printers	17,730.50	USD		
5000	3	50	700400	G/L Realized FX Curr	308.90-	USD	5000102001	500040

Figure 5.21: Exchange gain on the payment

This exchange gain has gone to the default profit center assigned to this account in 3KEH. However, the profit centers on the original invoice need to get their proportional share of this gain. To achieve this, run the periodic transaction F.50 P&L adjustment (see Figure 5.22). This transaction should be run at period end as it is specifically for adjusting cash discount and exchange rate postings between profit centers.

Profit and Loss Adjustment

Company Code	5000	to	
Document Number		to	

Selection of clearing procedures to be included

Reporting year	2016		
Reporting period	1	to	2

Control
- ☑ Process cash dscnts
- ☑ Process exch.rate differences

Posting parameters
- ☐ Create batch input session

Document Type	P0
Batch input session name	SAPF181

Figure 5.22: Initial screen profit and loss adjustment

On the initial screen, enter or select your `company code(s)`, the `reporting year`, the `reporting periods`, and whether you want to `process cash discounts`, `process exchange rate differences`, or both. For posting, you have to `create a batch input session`. If you do not select this parameter, then when you execute, there is only a test run. For the batch input, you need a document type and you can accept the default name. When you run F.50 and process the batch input session, it completes the profit center adjustment posting, as seen in Figure 5.23. The adjustment of cash discounts works in a similar manner.

```
Smarter Sisters US                    Chicago
Chicago
```

Text				
CoCd	DocumentNo	Year	Document Header Text	Pstng
G/L		Profit Ctr	Amount in LC	
Distribution of exchange rate difference				
5000			P&L adjustment	29.02
700400	500040		74.14	
700400	500010		74.14-	
700400	500040		49.42	
700400	500020		49.42-	
700400	500040		185.34	
700400	500030		185.34-	

Figure 5.23: Result of F.50.

5.2 Manual posting in classic PCA

One benefit of classic profit center accounting being a statistical component and being isolated in its own ledger is that you can make manual postings directly to classic PCA without worrying about it affecting other modules. In addition, it is not necessary for the postings to balance. Depending on the document type used for the posting, you can deactivate the balance check so that SAP only issues a warning if you do not balance. The transaction for manual posting is 9KE0. To enter a document, you need to specify a layout on the initial screen (see Figure 5.24). There are a number of delivered layouts; you also have the option to configure one to your needs. You need a document type for PCA transactions, and again there is a delivered option, but you can also create more if required. (I have created a custom option that allows you to make an unbalanced posting after seeing a warning message.) Finally, you are required to enter the posting date for the document. When you click execute, you move to another screen to enter the variables. Enter the company code. From this screen, click on the overview button to go to the entry screen for the posting (see Figure 5.25).

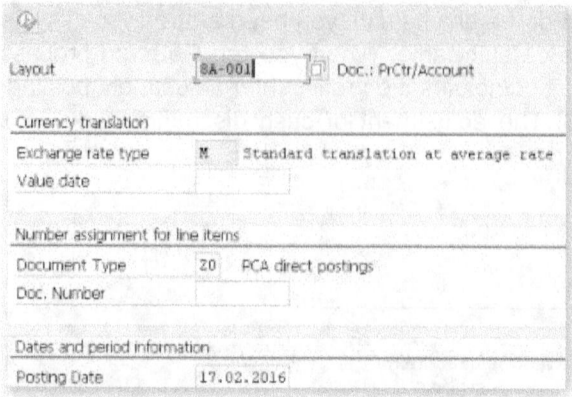

Figure 5.24: Profit center posting initial screen

Li...	Profit center	Account n...	In pctr local curr.	Unit
001	500040	750020	150,000.00	USD
002	500020	152000	10,000.00	USD
003	500030	152000	10,000.00-	USD

Figure 5.25: Create a PCA entry

In this case, move a prepaid expense between two profit centers and also make a one-sided entry to reflect a tax expense in profit center 500040. Note that there is no debit or credit indicator here, you have to use the sign of the transaction to indicate debit or credit. When you click the post 💾 button, you get a warning about the posting being unbalanced (see Figure 5.26), but due to the document type that you are using, you can continue to make a posting (see Figure 5.27).

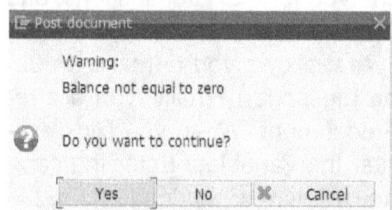

Figure 5.26: Out of balance warning message

```
Plan/Act./Var. w/o EIBV        Status:        17.02.2016Page:       2/    4

Controlling Area                              5000      Smarter Sisters
Profit Center/Group                           500040    US Corporate
Person responsible                            Charlie Brown
Reporting period            1      12         2016
```

Profit and loss accounts	Plan	Actual
750020 Corporate Income Tax Expense		150,000.00
* Total		150,000.00

Figure 5.27: Result of one-sided posting in PCA

Be careful with manual postings in PCA

 As you have seen, there are very few controls over the manual posting in PCA. It is possible to even deactivate the requirement for a document to balance. As these documents are only reflected in PCA and are not shown in other SAP modules, they can cause inconsistencies and confusion in reporting unless used with care.

Similar to what you saw in planning for classic PCA, you can perform assessments and distributions for actual values as well. The transactions are 3KE1 for assessment and 4KE1 for distribution. In general, these are only used for balance sheet items or P&L items that have been created without cost or revenue elements to avoid inconsistencies between CO and PCA.

5.3   Flow of actual values in the new GL

With profit center accounting in the new GL, you no longer use the separate 8A ledger for PCA. In fact, many separate ledgers that were used in the classic situation have been incorporated into the new GL (see Figure 5.28) in order to fulfil a number of identified business requirements (see Figure 5.29).

The profit center postings are now part of your standard general ledger document. This means that every actual transaction that flows into the GL can potentially have a profit center attached. In Section 1.3, you saw how the assignment of the scenarios FIN_PCA or FIN_SEGM to a ledger activate profit center accounting in the new GL. Refer back to Figure 1.2 to see where this is set up. For simplicity, only examples using one ledger are shown, but it is possible to have these scenarios activated in parallel ledgers.

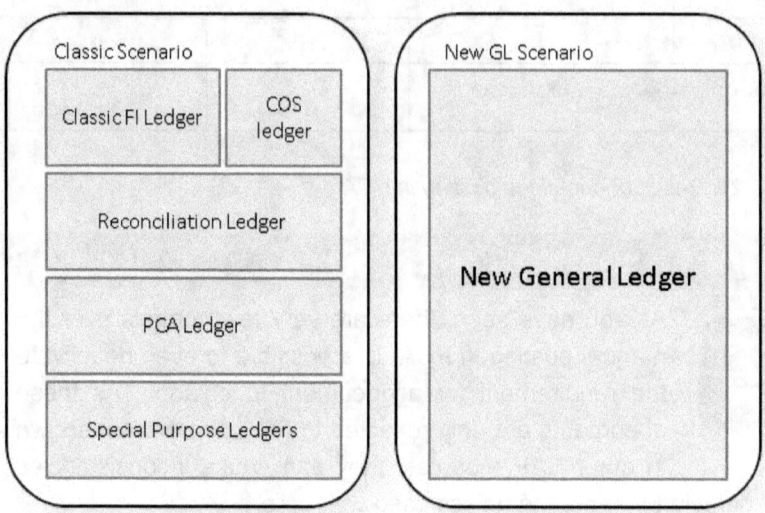

Figure 5.28: Classic scenario versus new GL

Figure 5.29: Benefits of the new GL

Since PCA is incorporated into the GL, you can essentially have all postings flowing to profit centers. For P&L items, the derivation of the profit center in the financial document is largely the same as for classic PCA. Most expense items derive the profit center from the associated cost object, such as the cost center or the order. Revenue and cost of sales postings still derive the profit center from the sales documents.

The big difference in the new GL is the treatment of balance sheet items and revenue and expense items that are either not CO relevant or need to be split, such as cash discount or expense items. The balance sheet items that you can transfer online in classic PCA—material stocks, WIP, and fixed assets—work similarly for the new GL since the profit center is derived based on assignment. If you require postings at the profit-center level for other items, such as payables and receivables, you need to activate document splitting and make some additional configuration settings.

The principle of online document splitting in the new GL is similar to what happened retroactively in classic PCA with the F.5D transaction. However, with document splitting activated in the new GL, this happens at the time of the posting rather than periodically. There is an example of this later, but first, look at the configuration settings that are relevant to profit center accounting and document splitting in the new GL. The overall configuration of document splitting is beyond the scope of this book and SAP provides wizards in configuration to guide you through the setup of document splitting and the creation of splitting rules if necessary. The important thing to look at is found in the IMG under SAP CUSTOMIZING IMPLEMENTATION GUIDE • FINANCIAL ACCOUNTING (NEW) • GENERAL LEDGER ACCOUNTING (NEW) • BUSINESS TRANSACTIONS • DOCUMENT SPLITTING • DEFINE DOCUMENT SPLITTING CHARACTERISTICS FOR GENERAL LEDGER ACCOUNTING (see Figure 5.30).

Here, you define the document splitting fields. In this case, use profit center and segment. You have two check boxes for each field that control a lot of the splitting behavior. The first box is `zero balance`; this tells the system that all postings involving that characteristic field must balance in a document. If you want to achieve a full trial balance by the characteristic, you set the `zero balance` check for that field. In order to achieve a zero balance on a characteristic, the system automatically generates additional line items in a document using clearing accounts.

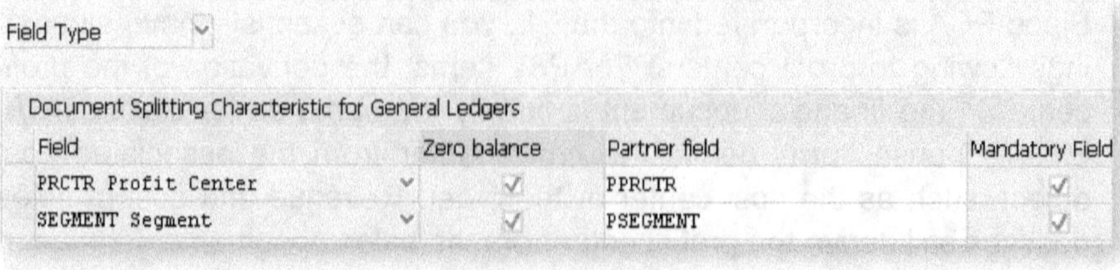

Field Type				
Document Splitting Characteristic for General Ledgers				
Field		Zero balance	Partner field	Mandatory Field
PRCTR Profit Center	✓	✓	PPRCTR	✓
SEGMENT Segment	✓	✓	PSEGMENT	✓

Figure 5.30: Document splitting characteristics for GL

The second check box is called `mandatory field`. Select this if you always want the field to have a value in it after document splitting occurs. Again, if you require a complete trial balance by the characteristic, select this option. Note that the configuration of document splitting and the set-up of the splitting rule control how the field gets populated after splitting, therefore, if there is a gap in this configuration, you may get errors on posting with this indicator set. The only option in this case is to fix the source of the problem in either the splitting rule or the configuration related to splitting and then try to re-post the document.

Once document splitting is activated, it is activated generally for the client; however, it is possible to deactivate splitting for individual company codes. The activation of splitting is done in SAP CUSTOMIZING IMPLEMENTATION GUIDE • FINANCIAL ACCOUNTING (NEW) • GENERAL LEDGER ACCOUNTING (NEW) • BUSINESS TRANSACTIONS • DOCUMENT SPLITTING • ACTIVATE DOCUMENT SPLITTING (see Figure 5.31). There are several things worth noting: in the DIALOG STRUCTURE, you have a sub-dialog to allow `deactivation per company code`; there is a check box to activate `document splitting`; and there is a `constant` for unassigned processes.

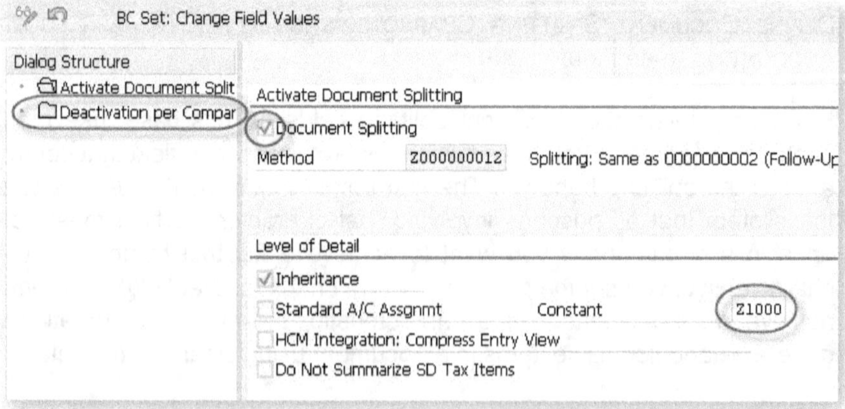

Figure 5.31: Activate document splitting

This last item requires a little more explanation. The constant is a default account assignment either for the segment or the profit center which is used when it is not possible to derive account assignments during posting. The constant is defined in SAP CUSTOMIZING IMPLEMENTATION GUIDE • FINANCIAL ACCOUNTING (NEW) • GENERAL LEDGER ACCOUNTING (NEW) • BUSINESS TRANSACTIONS • DOCUMENT SPLITTING • EDIT CONSTANTS FOR NONASSIGNED PROCESSES. There is one constant profit center defined per controlling area (see Figure 5.32). For a segment (not shown) there is one constant profit center for the whole client.

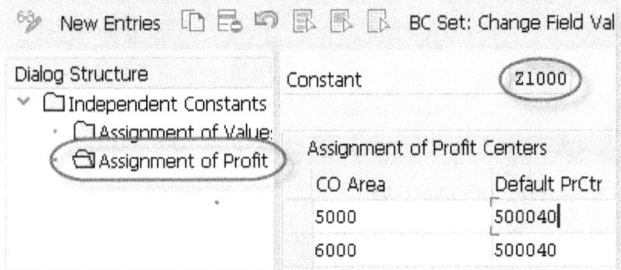

Figure 5.32: Constants for profit centers

The constant is not a dummy profit center and it is worth reiterating that a technical dummy profit center should not be defined for the new GL.

Within the new GL configuration, there is also a way to assign default profit centers to accounts by company code using transaction FAGL3KEH (see Figure 5.33). In the documentation for this configuration, SAP states that you should only use default profit centers for accounts that are not intended for document splitting.

Company Code	6000		
General Ledger: Default Profit Center			
Acct from	Account to	Def. PrCtr	
111000	111000	500040	
151000	152100	500040	
216000	216421	500040	

Figure 5.33: Assign default profit centers

127

As mentioned, any transactions involving material stocks, WIP, or fixed assets get a profit center assignment automatically. Next is a WIP example with the new GL. The production order shown in Figure 5.34 has not been fully delivered and has a cost balance (see Figure 5.35).

Order	1000007				Type	YI
Material	300004	Super Sergio Video Game			Plant	60
Status	REL PCNF PRC GMPS MACM PDLV SETC					

General	Assignment	Goods Receipt	Control	Dates/Qties	Master Data	Long Te

Quantities						
Total Qty	5,000	EA	Scrap Portion	0	0.00	%
Delivered	2,150		Short/Exc. Rcpt	0		

Figure 5.34: Partially delivered production order

Order	1000007 000000000000300004				
Order Type	YBM1 MTS Production Order				
Plant	6001 Indiana Mfg Plant				
Material	300004 Super Sergio Video Game				
Planned Quantity	5,000 EA each				
Actual Quantity	2,150 EA each				
Cost Elem.	Cost Element (Text)	Origin	Σ	Total act.costs	Currency
510000	Consumption - Raw Materials	6001/100074		6,968.64	USD
510010	Consumption - Semi Finished Goods	6001/200002		62,500.00	USD
510020	Consumption - Finished Goods	6001/300004		33,217.50-	USD
943000	Production Labour	5000101200/1000		1,760.00	USD
943010	Production Overhead	5000101200/1100		2,250.00	USD
				40,261.14	**USD**

Figure 5.35: Actual cost balance on production order

You don't want this cost balance on the P&L at the end of the period, so run the WIP analysis and post settlement to move this amount to the balance sheet (Figure 5.36). Since you are not using classic PCA, you only get a financial accounting document for this posting and the profit center is assigned as it was before.

PROFIT CENTER ACTUAL POSTINGS

Data Entry View				
Document Number	100000001	Company Code	6000	Fiscal Year	2016
Document Date	21.02.2016	Posting Date	29.02.2016	Period	2
Reference		Cross-Comp.No.		
Currency	USD	Texts exist		Ledger Group	

Co...	Itm	PK	Account	Description	Amount	Curr.	Profit Center
6000	1	50	539999	WIP Offset	40,261.14-	USD	500050
6000	2	40	136000	Inventory-WIP	40,261.14	USD	500050

Figure 5.36: New GL WIP posting

You see similar results for material postings and fixed asset postings.

You will start to see how document splitting works when you look at an AP or AR scenario. If you consider a vendor invoice with expenses going to a variety of cost objects assigned to different profit centers, you will see some differences with the new GL active. The first thing you should notice is that when you go into the document, you are taken to the *entry view*. This is the view of how the document was entered into the system by the accountant (see Figure 5.37). There is now a new button General Ledger View to take you to the view of the document after splitting has been applied. This new view is called the *general ledger view* (see Figure 5.38).

Data Entry View				
Document Number	1900000000	Company Code	6100	Fiscal Year	2016
Document Date	07.02.2016	Posting Date	07.02.2016	Period	2
Reference	9389208	Cross-Comp.No.		
Currency	CAD	Texts exist		Ledger Group	

Co...	Itm	PK	Account	Description	Amount	Curr.	Tx	Cost Center	Profit Cente
6100	1	31	100031	Counter feet printers	11,300.00-	CAD	PH		
6100	2	40	582020	Advertising	7,000.00	CAD	PH	5000114001	510030
6100	3	40	582020	Advertising	3,000.00	CAD	PH	5000114003	510020
6100	4	40	122000	CDN GST/HST Recov...	1,300.00	CAD	PH		

Figure 5.37: AP invoice showing entry view

129

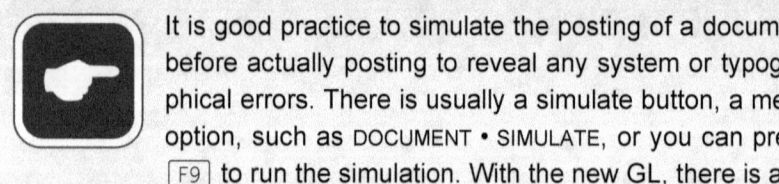

Figure 5.38: AP invoice showing general ledger view

You will notice two things. First, all the items that did not have a profit center in the entry view have been split between profit centers based on the proportion of the expense, and second, the AP splitting is occurring at the level of the reconciliation account not at the level of the vendor line item. Vendor line item reports are not split by profit center.

> **Posting simulation**
>
> It is good practice to simulate the posting of a document before actually posting to reveal any system or typographical errors. There is usually a simulate button, a menu option, such as DOCUMENT • SIMULATE, or you can press [F9] to run the simulation. With the new GL, there is also an additional option under the DOCUMENT menu called SIMULATE GE-NERAL LEDGER, or you can press [F12]. This option simulates the document splitting and reveals how the document will look after splitting.

This allows you to outline another difference that occurs with the new GL. In the classic GL, many of the reconciliation accounts were set to not allow line item display on the understanding that the details for these accounts would be available in the relevant sub-ledgers. With the new GL, line item display is now available on those reconciliation accounts and it shows the difference between the entry posting in the sub-ledger and the split posting in the general ledger.

```
Vendor          100031
Company Code    6100
Name            Counter feet printers
City            Windsor
```

S	DocumentNo	Account	Doc. Type	Doc. Date	Σ	Amount in local cur.	LCurr	Σ	Amount in loc.curr.2	LCur2	Profit Center
	1900000000	100031	KR	07.02.2016		11,300.00-	CAD		8,014.19-	USD	
		100031				11,300.00-	CAD		8,014.19-	USD	
						11,300.00-	CAD		8,014.19-	USD	

Figure 5.39: Vendor line item—not split

```
G/L Account     211000 Trade Payables
Company Code    6100
Ledger          0L
```

S	Documen...	Ty...	Doc. Date	PK	Σ	Amount in local cur.	LCurr	Σ	Amount in loc.curr.2	LCur2	Profit Center	Segment
	1900000000	KR	07.02.2016	31		3,390.00-	CAD		2,404.26-	USD	510020	5100
		KR	07.02.2016	31		7,910.00-	CAD		5,609.93-	USD	510030	5200
						11,300.00-	CAD		8,014.19-	USD		
Account 211000						11,300.00-	CAD		8,014.19-	USD		
						11,300.00-	CAD		8,014.19-	USD		

Figure 5.40: GL line item—split

The vendor line item (Figure 5.39) reflects the entry view of the document. Notice that there is no profit center available in this line. The GL line item (Figure 5.40) reflects the view in the GL payables reconciliation account after document splitting. Notice two line items and a profit center assignment.

Document splitting can also handle cash discounts and exchange-rate-difference scenarios that were processed with F.50 in the classic GL. For example, pay a $10,000 invoice with a 2% discount in the payment terms. The original AP invoice was split between two profit centers. The bank and discount postings are also split (see Figure 5.41).

Document Date		22.02.2016		Posting Date	22.02.2016	Fiscal Year		2016	
C...	Itm	L.item	PK	S G/L Account	G/L account name	Amount	Curr.	Profit Center	Segment
60...	1	000001	50	113105	CIBC US$-Checks Out	3,920.00-	USD	500010	5000
	1	000002	50	113105	CIBC US$-Checks Out	5,880.00-	USD	500030	5200
	2	000003	50	700210	Discount Received	120.00-	USD	500030	5200
	3	000004	50	700210	Discount Received	80.00-	USD	500010	5000
	4	000005	25	211000	TradeAP	4,000.00	USD	500010	5000
	4	000006	25	211000	TradeAP	6,000.00	USD	500030	5200

Figure 5.41: AP payment with discount split

Taking it to the next step, clear the payment either manually or through a bank statement upload. This results in another posting between the bank checks out account and the main bank account. This posting also gets split between the same two profit centers (see Figure 5.42).

Ledger 0L

Doc.		2000000000		FiscalYear		2016	Period	2
Co...	Itm	L.item	PK	Account	Description	Amount	Currency	Profit Center
6000	1	000001	50	113100	Bank CIBC US$	3,920.00-	USD	500010
6000	1	000002	50	113100	Bank CIBC US$	5,880.00-	USD	500030
6000	2	000003	40	113105	CIBC US$-Checks Out	3,920.00	USD	500010
6000	2	000004	40	113105	CIBC US$-Checks Out	5,880.00	USD	500030

Figure 5.42: Clearing the checks out account with split

Similar splitting happens on the AR side with a customer invoice, cash receipt, and cash clearance. Although there may still be transactions where you have to manually enter a profit center into a posting document, you can see how the online document splitting function in the new GL is a major improvement in achieving balanced statements by either profit center or segment.

Actual allocations are also available in the new GL. You can use FAGL-GA15 for actual assessment and FAGLGA35 for actual distribution. Because of the real-time integration between CO and FI, you should try to achieve all of your necessary allocations in CO and only use FI allocations if absolutely necessary. As with the actual allocations in classic PCA, the values posted here only remain in FI and do not flow back to CO.

5.4 Actual statistical key figures

You saw in planning that key figure postings to CO objects will flow into both classic PCA and the new GL. This is also the case for actual SKF postings. For classic PCA, this is controlled by the 3KEG settings shown in Section 2.7. For the new GL, this happens because of the online integration between CO and FI.

PROFIT CENTER ACTUAL POSTINGS

As an example, consider a marketing order to track sales leads. Create the SKF LEADS and post some values to it in CO using transaction KB31N (see Figure 5.43).

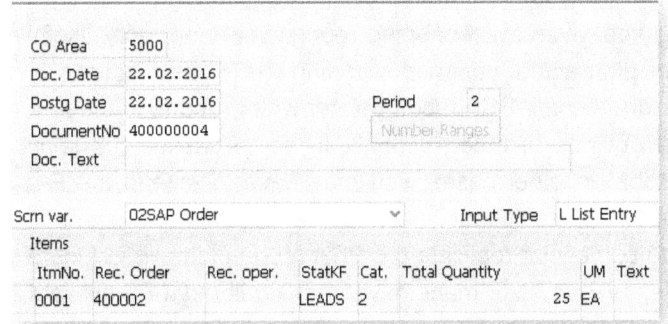

Figure 5.43: Actual SKF posting into internal order in CO

In the standard PCA report S_ALR_87013342 – Profit Center: Statistical Key Figures, this posting has transferred into PCA (see Figure 5.44). Figure 5.45 shows the same data in the new GL.

Stat. Key Figures Controlling Area		Date: 23.02.2016 5000 Smarter Sisters		Page: 2 / 3	
Profit Center Group Fiscal Year From Period To Period		500030 2016	Card Games - US		
Statistical key figures	Actual		Plan	Var. (abs.)	Var. (%)
1 January	35		40	5-	13-
2 February	25		40	15-	38-
* 3 Overhead Cost Order	60		80	20-	25-
** LEADS Leads Generated	60		80	20-	25-

Figure 5.44: Stat key figures in PCA

GL-SKF Report Company Code		23.02.2016 5000 Smarter Sisters US		Page : 1 / 1	
Profit Center / Group (1 From Period Plan Version	1 0	500030 2016 To Period	Card Games - US 2		
Statistical Key Figures	Actual		Plan	Var. (abs)	Var. (%)
1 January	35		40	5-	13-
2 February	25		40	15-	38-
* LEADS Leads Generated	60		80	20-	25-
** Total	60		80	20-	25-

Figure 5.45: Stat key figures in the new GL

> ### SKF reporting in the new GL
>
>
> Reporting on SKFs is very limited in the standard reports in the new GL. The transaction FAGLSKF3—Period Evaluation gives a list-oriented report, but is not very useful for plan actual variance reporting. SAP has functions to migrate some PCA report painter/writer reports to the new GL. These are outlined in note 1555535. In some cases, it is fairly straightforward, but in other cases, you may have to extend the FAGLFLEXT table to add additional fields. You can also create reports in report painter to somewhat replicate the PCA reports (shown in Figure 5.45). As of release 6.04, SAP made new reporting library 0FS available, which can be used to build SKF reports in the new GL.

It is also possible to manually enter SKF values into either the classic PCA or the new GL using the following transactions:

- Classic PCA – 9KE5 – Change
- New GL – FAGLSKF – Post (Actual)

Imagine a requirement to track the number of individual products that each division markets to its customers. For example, in the U.S., the company currently sells 36 different board games. Use SKFs at the profit-center level to track this as it is not relevant information for the cost center managers.

Posting actual SKF values in 9KE5 appears almost like a planning transaction (see Figure 5.46). You must select a `layout`. The type of layout depends on whether you are entering postings for a type 1 or type 2 statistic (refer back to Section 2.7 if you don't remember the difference). Then enter a `document type` and click the button. On the next screen, enter the characteristics (not shown) similar to a planning characteristics screen. Enter the relevant characteristics for the posting such as; `periods, year, company code, profit center,` and `statistical key figure` and then click either the button or the button to go to the posting screen (see Figure 5.47) where you enter the statistical values.

The posting in FAGLSKF is easier. Simply enter the transaction; if the layout is not appropriate for what you want, then click on the `Switch Layout` button and choose from the list. With the correct layout in place, enter your values (see Figure 5.48) and post.

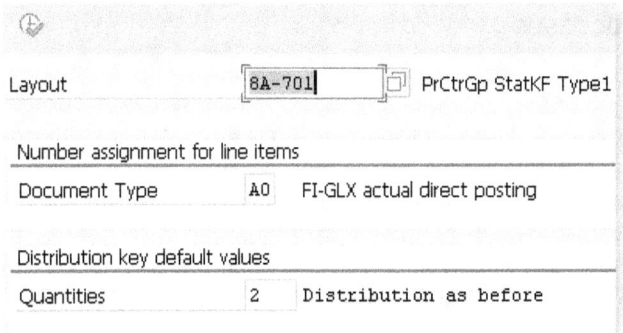

Figure 5.46: Enter actual SKF in PCA initial screen

Fiscal Year	2016		
Period	1	To	1
Company Code	5000		Smarter Sisters US
Statistical key fig.	PRODLI		Number of Products

Profit center	Text	Quantity	Dis...	Unit
500010	Video Games - US	12	2	EA
500020	Board Games - US	36	2	EA
500030	Card Games - US	102	2	EA
*Profit ce	Total	150		

Figure 5.47: Posting actual SKF in classic PCA

Header Data

CoCode	5000	Smarter Sisters US
Date From	31.01.2016	
Date To	31.01.2016	
Layout	01 Profit Center	

Item Data

Profit Center	StatKF	C	Quantity	Unit
500010	PRODLI	1	12	EA
500020	PRODLI	1	36	EA
500030	PRODLI	1	102	EA

Figure 5.48: Posting actual SKF in new GL

These actual SKFs can be used in reports or as the *tracing factors* in assessments or distributions in the classic PCA or the new GL.

5.5 Periodic processes

One of SAP's outlined benefits of the new GL is a faster and less complicated closing process. You have already seen that there are some periodic processes required for classic PCA, such as running the balance sheet and P&L adjustments transactions and performing the transfer of payables and receivables, which are no longer required in the new GL. In addition to simply doing away with the transactions, there is also the benefit of all the data residing in one ledger, which should also eliminate reconciliation efforts.

Along with the monthly periodic processes in PCA, there is also the annual process, balance carry forward transaction 2KES, which carries the balances forward into a new fiscal year. This is another step that can be eliminated with the new GL as it is now covered by the GL balance carry forward transaction FAGLGVTR.

Within the new GL, there is nothing additional that needs to be done from a periodic closing perspective to accommodate profit center accounting. All the normal GL period-end and year-end activities that are normally run still apply. The only possible addition is if assessments or distributions are required at the profit center or segment level, then these would have to be accommodated into the month-end schedule.

5.6 Summary

In this chapter, you learned about the flow of actual postings into PCA in both the classic and the new GL scenarios. In the classic PCA example, you saw how some balance sheet items can be automatically transferred online into PCA while others require periodic transfer or manual intervention. You learned how the assignment of profit centers to other objects, such as materials, cost centers, or assets actually flow into the postings created for those objects. You saw that in classic PCA, it is possible to make manual postings directly to the PCA ledger without impacting either the GL or other parts of controlling. In the new GL example, you learned about the concept of document splitting and how it can be configured to affect postings to profit centers. Finally, you looked at the difference in periodic processes between classic PCA and the new GL.

6 Profit center transfer pricing

In this chapter, I explain the concept of transfer pricing and show how it can be applied within profit center accounting. The concept of transfer pricing is fairly easy to explain and understand, but the configuration and setup required to activate it in the system is fairly extensive and goes across multiple areas of FICO, including activating the material ledger. For that reason, there are a number of configuration-related screens shown before the examples.

6.1 Transfer pricing scenarios in SAP

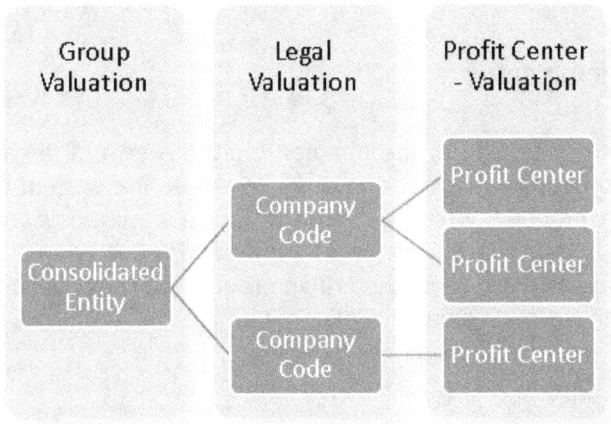

Figure 6.1: Levels of valuation in SAP

Due to varying different requirements around transfer pricing, SAP allows some flexibility in defining how it is going to work (see Figure 6.1). Most often, you work with the idea of legal valuation since this defines the valuation of materials for legal purposes at the company-code level. However, if you think of multiple companies belonging to a consolidated group, you may also be interested in group valuation. From a legal, and often a tax perspective, it is necessary for related companies to buy from and sell to each other using a transfer price. This is a price that includes the cost of the goods being transferred and an additional markup to provide a profit for the selling company. At a group level, you are not interested in the cost of the materials that includes all of the inter-company markups. You are only interested in the group valuation.

In the profit center valuation scenario, you are interested in looking at the profitability of each responsibility area. If profit centers belong to the same company code and they supply goods to each other, you want to apply transfer pricing so that each profit center can be evaluated as a standalone business.

> **Profit center assignment**
>
>  Profit centers are generally portrayed as being contained within a company code, but that is not necessarily always the case. Profit centers can be assigned to more than one company code, as you saw in Figure 2.9.

6.2 Transfer pricing setup

As mentioned at the beginning of the chapter, there are several areas where configuration needs to be done in order to set up the system to use transfer pricing properly. First, you need to define a currency and valuation profile in transaction 8KEM (see Figure 6.2). In this example, only profit center valuation will be defined. If you require group valuation, add another line with a group valuation view.

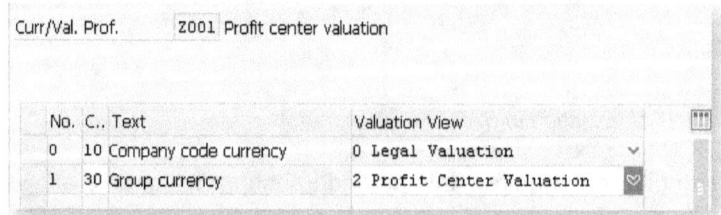

Figure 6.2: Valuation profile

Next, assign the profile to your controlling area in transaction 8KEQ (see Figure 6.3).

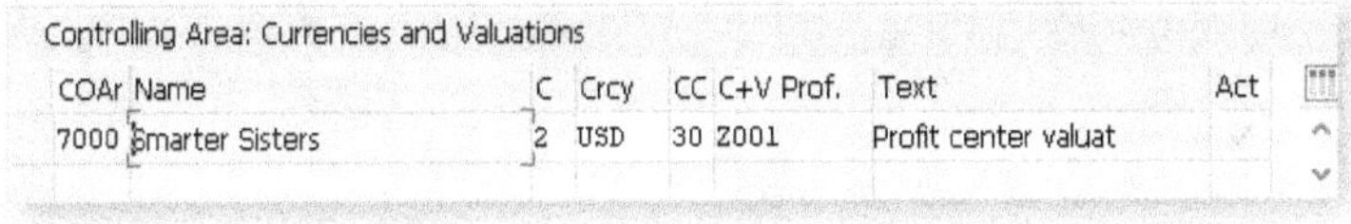

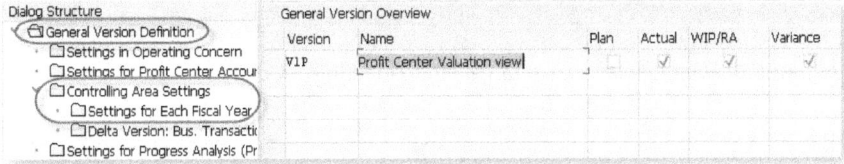

Figure 6.3: Assign currency and valuation to controlling area

In order to store different valuations in your controlling area, you need to create up to two delta versions in OKEQ for both the general controlling level and the controlling area level. Version 0 is used for legal valuation, so depending on whether you want a group and/or a profit center valuation, you will create up to two more versions (see Figure 6.4).

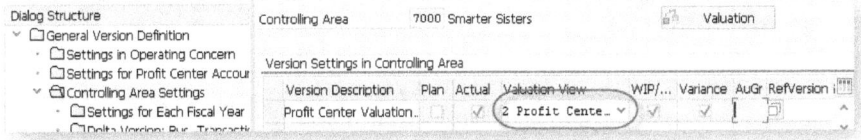

Figure 6.4: New version for profit center valuation

At the controlling area level, you need to assign the valuation view for this version (see Figure 6.5).

Figure 6.5: New version controlling area settings

Also in the GL configuration, you need to check the parallel currency setup for your company codes for the leading ledger in OB22. One of the parallel currency valuation views should equate to the valuation view being tracked (see Figure 6.6). If you are using classic PCA, then you also need to make some changes in the controlling area settings in transaction OKE5. Set the VALUATION VIEW to Profit Center Valuation (see Figure 6.7). You may have to disable the STORE IN TRANSACTION CURRENCY check box as this setting is incompatible with profit center valuation.

1st local currency				
Crcy type	10	Company code currency	Currency	USD
Valuation	0	Legal Valuation		
ExRateType	M	Standard translation at average rate		
Srce curr.	1	Translation taking transaction currency as a basis		
TrsDte typ	3	Translation date		

2nd local currency				
Crcy type	30	Group currency	Currency	USD
Valuation	2	Profit Center Valuation		
ExRateType	M	Standard translation at average rate		
Srce curr.	2	Translation taking first local currency as a basis		
TrsDte typ	3	Translation date		

Figure 6.6: Parallel currency and valuation in leading ledger

Controlling Area	7000	Smarter Sisters
Controlling Area Settings		
Dummy Profit Center	DUMMY	DUMMY PC
Standard Hierarchy	5000	Smarter Sisters
Elim. of Int. Business Vol.	✓	
PCtr Local Currency Type	20	Controlling area currency
Profit Center Local Currency	USD	
Store Transaction Currency	☐	
Valuation View	2 Profit Center Valuation	
ALE Distribution Method	No distribution to other systems	

Figure 6.7: Controlling area settings for classic PCA

At this point, it is necessary to configure and activate the material ledger (which isn't shown in detail) and then activate the currency and valuation profile using transaction 8KEP (see Figure 6.8). Run this in CHECK ACTIVATION mode first to check if your entire configuration is consistent and to get a report showing any incomplete items.

The next step in PCA configuration is to define the account determination for internal goods movements in transaction 0KEK (see Figure 6.9). Here, you need to define the accounts to be used for inter-profit center revenue and cost of sales. You can define different account determinations based on material type, valuation class, and valuation area grouping code. The account that you define for INTERNAL REV will receive the revenue posting in the profit center valuation view and the CHG STOCK account will receive the cost of sales posting in the profit center view.

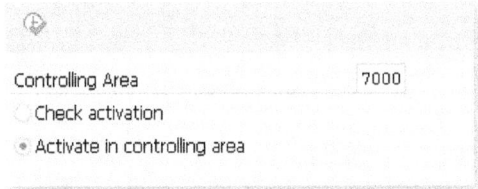

Controlling Area   7000
   Check activation
• Activate in controlling area

Figure 6.8: Activate currency and valuation profile

New Entries

CO Area	7000	Smarter Sisters					
Matl Type	ValCl		VGCd	No re...	Internal rev.	Chg. stock	Delivery
FERT	3520		0001	✓	695000	695100	

Figure 6.9: Account determination for profit center transfer price

Following that, you need to maintain the transfer price variant in transaction 8KEZ. SAP provides a number of condition types and pricing procedures that you can use in your transfer price variant or you can create your own custom pricing procedures. The step shown in Figure 6.10 is simply creating the transfer price variant by linking it to a predefined pricing procedure. The actual pricing is maintained based on the condition types. The example uses condition type TP02 to assign a markup percentage to the materials. When you create pricing here, you need to select an *access sequence* to control the level of the pricing (see Figure 6.11). Then you can maintain the actual percentage markups based on the access that you choose (see Figure 6.12).

Controlling Area	7000	
Trans. Price Variant	000	Profit Center Price
Condition Analysis		

Transfer price variants

No.	Proc.	Description		Or
1	TP0002	Transfer prices - percentage		00

Figure 6.10: Create transfer price variant

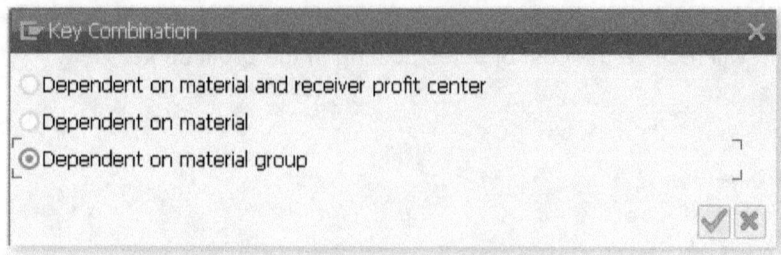

Figure 6.11: Select access sequence for transfer pricing

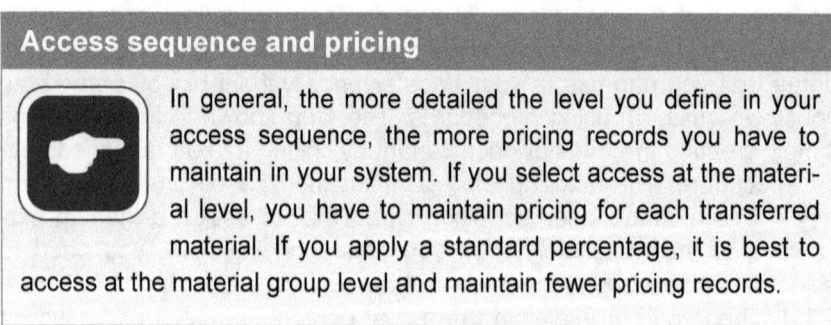

Figure 6.12: Percentage markups by material group

> ### Access sequence and pricing
>
> In general, the more detailed the level you define in your access sequence, the more pricing records you have to maintain in your system. If you select access at the material level, you have to maintain pricing for each transferred material. If you apply a standard percentage, it is best to access at the material group level and maintain fewer pricing records.

That is it for PCA configuration, but as mentioned, this goes across modules in FICO, so you are not finished yet. The next area to look at is product costing. Consider a requirement to have two cost valuations on the material master. If you are using standard costing with a quantity structure, you need to create, mark, and release cost estimates to get that standard cost updated on the material master. With legal valuation, you updated a standard cost in the legal view, but now you may need to update standard costs in the profit center valuation view and/or the group valuation view. For each different valuation view that you have, you need to perform a separate *costing run* and in each costing run you need to have a different *costing variant*.

The costing variant is a grouping of other configuration elements related to costing, so when you build the costing variant you need to configure the other elements first. The first item is the *costing type*. This is used to define the purpose of the cost estimate. Define a costing type for each type of valuation. Costing type P1 for profit center valuation is defined in Figure 6.13 and Figure 6.14.

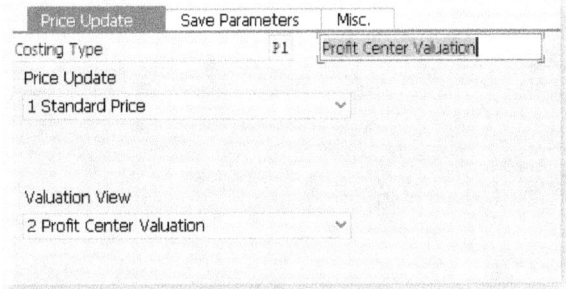

Figure 6.13: Costing type P1 price update tab

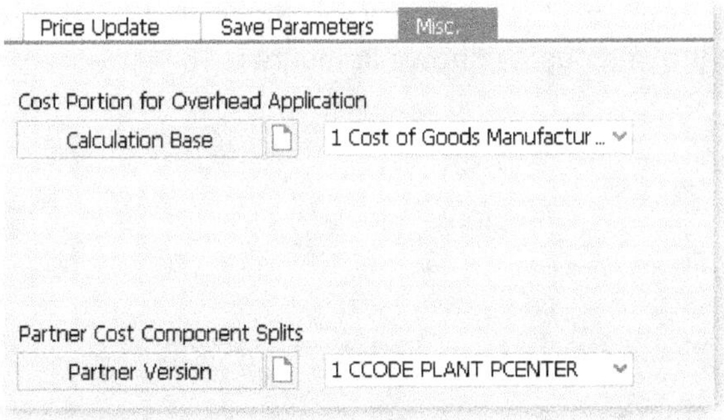

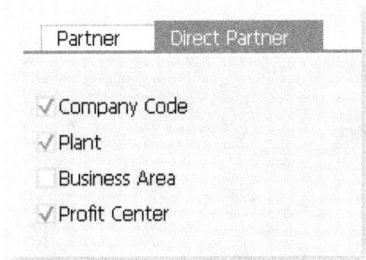

Figure 6.14: Costing type Misc tab

While you are in here, create the PARTNER VERSION and complete the settings on the DIRECT PARTNER tab (see Figure 6.15).

Figure 6.15: Partner version direct partner tab

143

Next, configure a *transfer control* to tell the system to use your legal costing variant as the basis for your additional valuation. An example of transfer control TP01 for profit center transfer pricing is shown in Figure 6.16. Transfer from whatever costing variant you are using for your legal standard costings. This example uses YPC1.

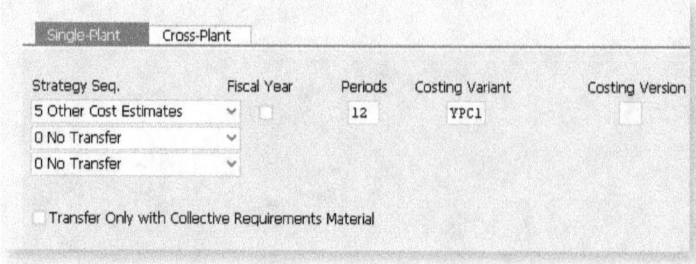

Figure 6.16: Transfer control TP01

Next, define a *reference variant* to tell the system to use the quantity structure of an existing cost estimate. On the COST ESTIMATE REF tab, assign the TRANSFER CONTROL that you created previously (see Figure 6.17) and on the revaluation tab, make the settings as shown in Figure 6.18.

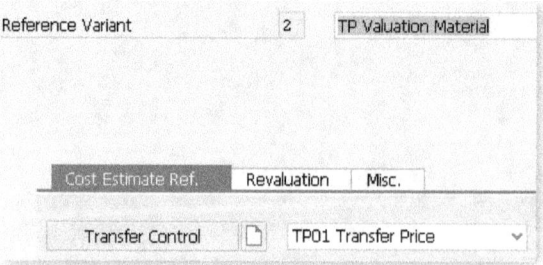

Figure 6.17: Reference variant assign transfer control

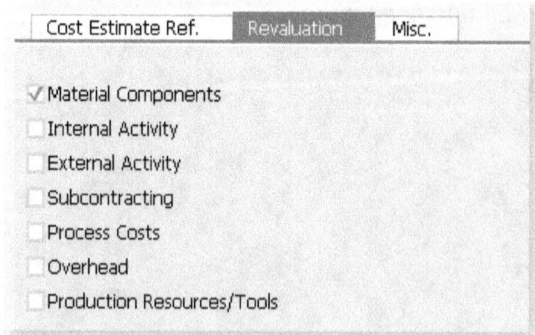

Figure 6.18: Reference variant revaluation settings

144

After completing the reference variant, you should create *costing versions* in transaction OKYD. Versions normally enable you to save multiple versions of cost estimates for the same material and costing variant. In this case, you need the version to assign your TRANSFER PRICE VARIANT ❶ to your COSTING TYPE ❷ (see Figure 6.19).

Costing Version	Costing Type	Valuation Variant	Varian...	Exch. ...	Qty St...	Description
1	01	Y01				Cost version legal view
1	P1 ❷		0 ❶			Cost version prcnt view

Figure 6.19: Costing versions

Depending on requirements, you may also need to update your cost component structure to include a delta cost component for the transfer price surcharge (not shown).

Finally, tie all this together in the costing variant. Create your new costing variant and assign the COSTING TYPE ❶ that you created. Use the same VALUATION VARIANT, DATE CONTROL, and QUANTITY STRUCTURE CONTROL ❷ that you used in your costing variant for legal valuation and assign your REFERENCE VARIANT ❸. It is not necessary to assign the transfer control as it is contained in the reference variant already.

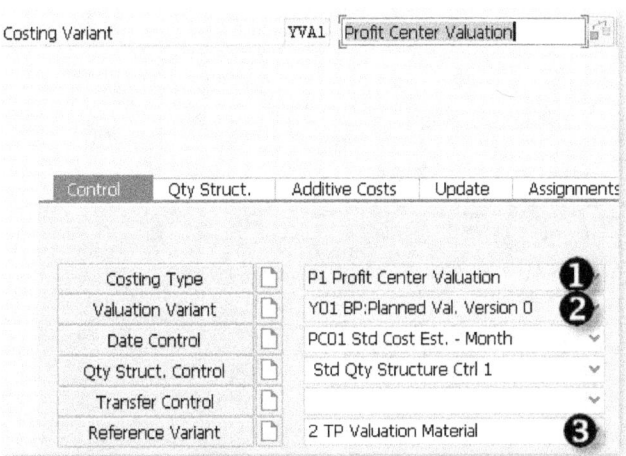

Figure 6.20: Costing variant for profit center valuation

There are some areas of configuration that are not shown in detail as they do not directly impact the example shown. In a manufacturing environment with production orders, you have to configure additional results analysis versions to calculate the WIP in the parallel valuation views. In

145

addition, if you are using costing-based COPA, there will be more configuring to be done to have your transfer pricing reflected in your operating concern. It is not shown here as it does not stop you from learning the inter-profit center scenario.

6.3 Transfer pricing in practice

Once your costing configuration is done and you create your relevant master data, you can see the result of this configuration on your materials and on your transactions. The scenario that follows is fairly simple (see Figure 6.21).

In plant 7002, make a component to transfer to plant 7001. This component is used to make a finished product and then will be transferred to plant 7000, a distribution center that will sell the finished product to a customer. When the component is transferred from plant 7002 to plant 7001 there is a 15% markup in profit center valuation based on the pricing conditions that you saw in Figure 6.12. That product is used in finished good 30007, resulting in a difference between the legal valuation and the profit center valuation (see Figure 6.22).

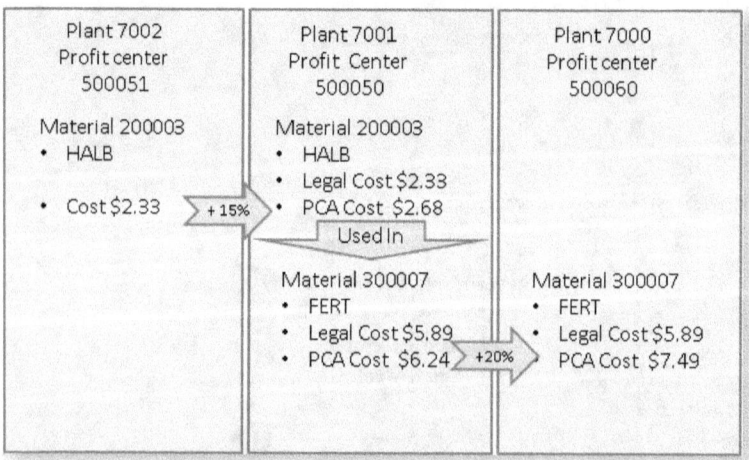

Figure 6.21: Simple transfer price scenario

This finished material is then sent to the distribution center, plant 7000, with an additional 20% markup in profit center valuation. Notice that the legal valuation does not change because the two plants are in the same company code (see Figure 6.23).

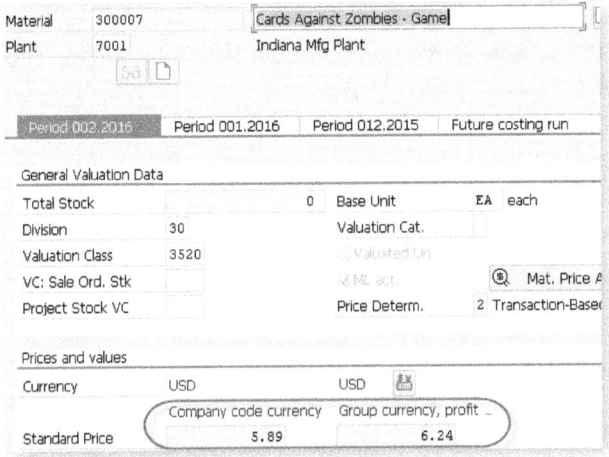

Figure 6.22: Finished material in plant 7001

Legal valuation by plant

 Costing is usually plant specific in SAP, so it is possible to have different legal valuations by plant. This results in a transfer variance posting when the materials are moved between different plants. This occurs whether the plants belonged to different profit centers or not.

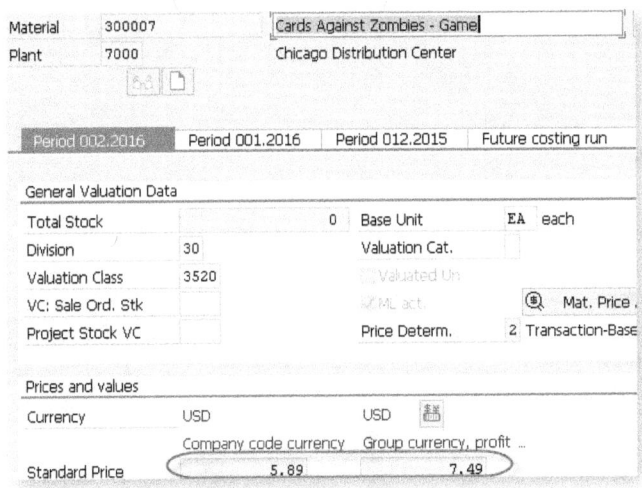

Figure 6.23: Finished material in plant 7000

Because you have this valuation in parallel, you can see postings happening with respect to material movements in both valuation areas. This is true for both classic PCA and for the new GL. To illustrate how this works, look at a simple plant to plant transfer of the finished goods material (see Figure 6.24).

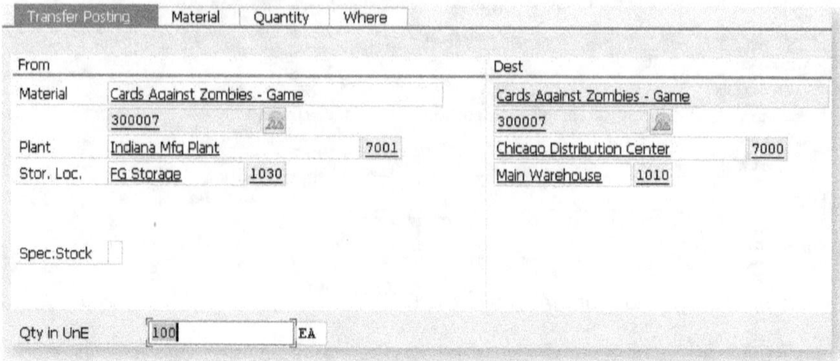

Transfer Posting	Material	Quantity	Where			
From				**Dest**		
Material	Cards Against Zombies - Game			Cards Against Zombies - Game		
	300007			300007		
Plant	Indiana Mfg Plant		7001	Chicago Distribution Center		7000
Stor. Loc.	FG Storage	1030		Main Warehouse	1010	
Spec.Stock						
Qty in UnE	100	EA				

Figure 6.24: Material transfer plant to plant

This material is linked to different profit centers on the plant-specific views for plants 7001 and 7000, so by moving the material across plants you triggered a revenue and cost of sales posting in the profit center valuation view. The profit center document in Figure 6.25 shows the inventory being received in profit center 500060 at the marked up value. In profit center 500050, you see the revenue and cost of sales posting as well as the inventory being relieved at the profit center value in plant 7001.

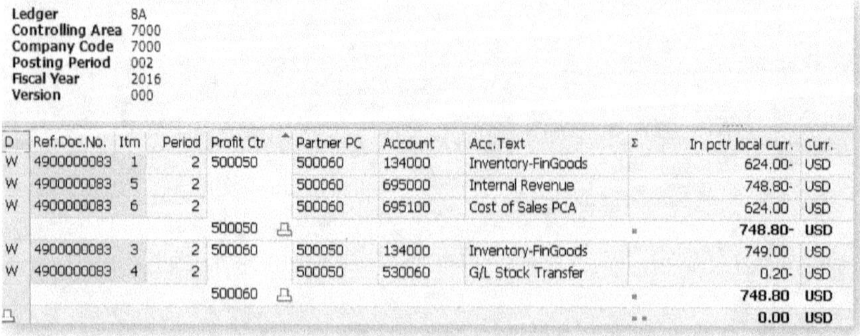

```
Ledger            8A
Controlling Area  7000
Company Code      7000
Posting Period    002
Fiscal Year       2016
Version           000
```

D	Ref.Doc.No.	Itm	Period	Profit Ctr	Partner PC	Account	Acc.Text	Σ	In pctr local curr.	Curr.
W	4900000083	1	2	500050	500060	134000	Inventory-FinGoods		624.00-	USD
W	4900000083	5	2		500060	695000	Internal Revenue		748.80-	USD
W	4900000083	6	2		500060	695100	Cost of Sales PCA		624.00	USD
				500050				•	748.80-	USD
W	4900000083	3	2	500060	500050	134000	Inventory-FinGoods		749.00	USD
W	4900000083	4	2		500050	530060	G/L Stock Transfer		0.20-	USD
				500060				•	748.80	USD
								••	0.00	USD

Figure 6.25: PCA posting from material transfer

PROFIT CENTER TRANSFER PRICING

If you look at the GL accounting document, you can see the legal view of this transaction (see Figure 6.26). You can see that it is a debit and credit to inventory in the two profit centers.

Co...	Itm	PK	Account	Description	Amount	Curr.	Profit Center	Material	Plant
7000	1	99	134000	Inventory-FinGoods	589.00-	USD	500050	300007	7001
7000	2	89	134000	Inventory-FinGoods	589.00	USD	500060	300007	7000
7000	3	93	530060	G/L Stock Transfer	0.00	USD	500060	300007	7000
7000	4	50	695000	Internal Revenue	0.00	USD	500050	300007	7001
7000	5	40	695100	Cost of Sales PCA	0.00	USD	500050	300007	7001

Figure 6.26: Accounting document legal view

If you click on the Display Currency button, you have the option to view the document differently (see Figure 6.27).

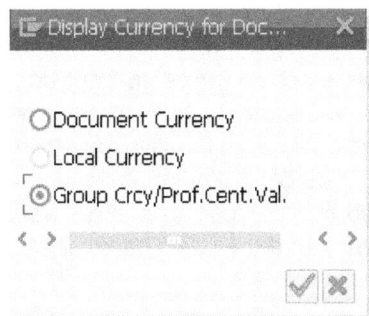

Figure 6.27: Select currency and valuation for document display

The document is displayed based on profit center valuation (see Figure 6.28) and will look similar to what you saw in the profit center document.

In classic PCA, you have profit center documents posting based on the profit center valuation. In the new GL, you have documents posting with both valuations and you can toggle back and forth between views. When running reports in the new GL, you can select and display the reports in the correct currency and valuation.

149

Data Entry View									
Document Number	4900000016		Company Code		7000		Fiscal Year		2016
Document Date	24.02.2016		Posting Date		24.02.2016		Period		2
Reference			Cross-Comp.No.						
Currency	USD		Texts exist				Ledger Group		

CoCd	Itm	PK	Account	Description	Σ	Amount	Curr.	Profit Ctr	Material	Plant
7000	1	99	134000	Inventory-FinGoods		624.00-	USD	500050	300007	7001
7000	4	50	695000	Internal Revenue		748.80-	USD	500050	300007	7001
7000	5	40	695100	Cost of Sales PCA		624.00	USD	500050	300007	7001
						748.80-	USD	500050		
7000	2	89	134000	Inventory-FinGoods		749.00	USD	500060	300007	7000
7000	3	93	530060	G/L Stock Transfer		0.20-	USD	500060	300007	7000
						748.80	USD	500060		
						0.00	USD			

Figure 6.28: GL document in profit center valuation

6.4 Summary

In this chapter, you learned the basic concepts of transfer pricing in SAP and how transfer pricing can be used for either group valuation or for profit center valuation. You saw that there is considerable up-front configuration and setup to properly activate transfer pricing, but there is little additional effort from the end users once it is in place. Finally, you saw a simple example of transfer pricing and profit center valuation in action. In reality, scenarios and requirements around transfer pricing can get very complex; this was designed to show the setup and the basic capabilities.

7 Reporting in profit center accounting

In this chapter, I cover standard reporting for profit center accounting under the classic PCA and the new GL scenarios. I also explore some options for using the report painter and drilldown reporting tools for profit center reports under both situations.

7.1 Reporting in classic PCA

Classic PCA is a sub-module within controlling so it has its own information system tree in the SAP menu. A variety of standard profit center reports are provided. The information system for profit center accounting is divided into four sections (see Figure 7.1).

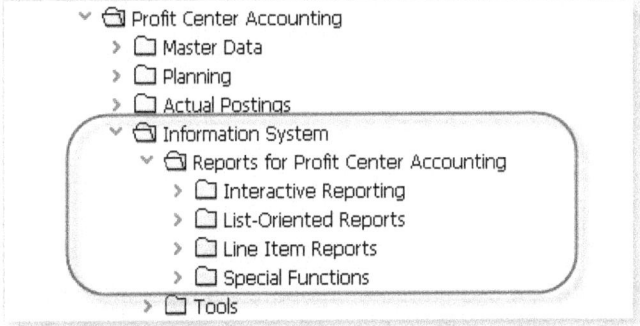

Figure 7.1: Classic PCA information system menu

Put reporting first

During the initial implementation of an SAP system, the project team often becomes extremely focused on meeting the functional requirements of the business through different configuration options and the reporting requirements are often left until later in the project. I feel that this is a mistake and, especially for the financial modules, the reporting requirements should be addressed as early in the project as possible.

151

The first two folders, INTERACTIVE REPORTING and LIST-ORIENTED REPORTS, appear to contain many similar reports (see Figure 7.2). The difference is in how the reports are built and how they are presented to the user. The reports in the INTERACTIVE REPORTING section are standard *drilldown reports* provided by SAP which will display an overview list at a general level first and then provide the user with the ability to display more detailed information. The LIST-ORIENTED REPORTS are standard *report painter* reports provided by SAP which exist in predefined report groups within report writer. They may also provide drilldown capability through a report-to-report interface to display more detailed line item reports.

Figure 7.2: Interactive and list-oriented reports for PCA

For the most part, these are designed as comparative reports that allow you to compare actual values versus plan values or compare actual or plan values between different periods.

The following are the interactive drilldown reports along with brief descriptions of the information they provide (as many of the reports are similar in layout, only the output and selection screen for the first report are shown, see Figure 7.3 and Figure 7.4):

- ▶ S_ALR_87013326 – Profit Center Group: Plan/Actual/Variance—allows you to display the plan versus actual values for a selected time period, plan version, profit center or group, and P&L account or group.
  - ▶ S_ALR_87013327 – Profit Center Comparison: Plan/Actual/Variance—allows you to compare the plan versus actual values for a selected time period, plan version, and P&L account or group for two selected profit centers.

- S_ALR_87013330 – Profit Center Group:
  Plan/Plan/Actual Versions — allows you to compare the plan versus actual values for a selected time period, profit center or group, and P&L account or group using two different plan versions.
- S_ALR_87013332 – Profit Center Group:
  Current Period/Aggregated/Year—allows you to display the plan versus actual values for a selected period and cumulatively to the selected period by plan version, profit center or group, and P&L account or group.
- S_ALR_87013334 – Profit Center Group:
  Compare Actual Quarters over two Years—shows quarterly actual values for two selected years based on profit center or profit center group and P&L account or account group.
- S_ALR_87013336 – Profit Center Group:
  Balance Sheet Accounts Plan/Actual/Variance—allows you to display the plan versus actual values for a selected time period, plan version, profit center or group, and balance sheet account or group.
- S_ALR_87013337 – Profit Center Group:
  Key Figures—allows you to display the plan versus actual values for a selected fiscal year plan version, profit center or group, P&L account group, and balance sheet account group for profit, fixed capital, profit adjusted for cost of capital (based on an entered rate), and return on investment (ROI).
- S_ALR_87013339 – Profit Center Comparison:
  Return on Investment—allows you to compare the actual and planned ROI between two selected profit centers based on selected P&L and balance sheet account groups.

> **Use profit center and account groups**
>
>
> One of the main purposes for groups in SAP is to help with reporting. Using structured profit center and/or account groups in reporting rather than just using a range of values allows you to see your reports based on the levels within the group structure. For example, I copied my account groups based on a financial statement version that I am using in FI so that I can display my profit center P&L and balance sheet with the same groupings that I have in the GL. You can see this in Figure 7.4.

Report selections		
From period	1	January
To period	2	February
Fiscal year	2016	2016
Plan version	0	Plan/actual version
Profit center group	5000	Smarter Sisters
Or values		to
Prof.+loss accts grp	PCA63.99	Income Before Taxes
Or values		to

Figure 7.3: Selection screen for interactive report

Header	Selection data	General Data Selection					
Controlling area	7000		Smarter Sisters				
	<>		<>				
	<>		<>				
Plan version	0		Plan/actual version				

Navigation	P	N	Account Number		Plan	Actual	Variance	Var. %
Account N			˅ PCA65.99	Gross Profit	44,875,000.00-	48,635,652.90-	3,760,652.90-	8.38029
Period			˅ PCA66.99	Net Sales	102,500,000.00-	94,676,500.00-	7,823,500.00	7.63268-
Profit Center			˅ PCA67.99	Revenue	102,500,000.00-	94,676,500.00-	7,823,500.00	7.63268-
Partner PC			· 410000	Sales Revenue	102,500,000.00-	94,676,500.00-	7,823,500.00	7.63268-
Company Code			˅ PCA79.99	Cost of Goods Sold	57,625,000.00	46,040,847.10	11,584,152.90-	20.10265-
Functional Are			> PCA69.99	Cost of Goods Sold	57,625,000.00	46,657,872.40	10,967,127.60-	19.03189-
Origin object			> PCA70.99	SAP Manufacturing Cl	0.00	8,002.78-	8,002.78-	x/o
Plant			> PCA71.99	Inventory Reserves	0.00	576,422.22-	576,422.22-	x/o
Rep. material			> PCA72.99	Manufacturing Varian	0.00	32,600.30-	32,600.30-	x/o
			˅ PCA84.99	Operating Expenses	33,791,333.36	32,092,677.63	1,698,655.73-	5.02690-
			˅ PCA73.99	Personnel Expense	10,786,666.66	10,616,799.62	169,867.04-	1.57479-
			· 540000	Salaries	9,286,666.66	9,201,640.00	85,026.66-	0.91558-
			· 540010	Labour-Reg-Productn	1,200,000.00	1,206,740.00	6,740.00	0.56167
			· 540015	Labour-OT-Production	300,000.00	208,419.62	91,580.38-	30.52679-
			˅ PCA75.99	Utilities	1,653,333.32	1,614,898.00	38,435.32-	2.32472-
			· 545000	Elect-Supply&Dist'n	833,333.33	756,856.00	76,477.33-	9.17728-

Figure 7.4: Interactive report S_ALR_87013326

The drilldown reports have several useful features worth reviewing. The navigation pane on the left, shown in Figure 7.4, allows you to select the characteristics for drilldown. For example, you can look at the detail of the sales revenue account by profit center (see Figure 7.5) and you can toggle between accounts by clicking on the ▲ ▼ buttons next to the account.

Navigation	P	N	Text	Profit Center		Plan	Actual	Variance	Var. %
Account N				˅ 5000	Smarter Sisters	102,500,000.00-	94,676,500.00-	7,823,500.00	7.63268-
· 410000	▲ ▼		Sales Revenue	· 500010	Video Games - US	40,000,000.00-	45,001,000.00-	5,001,000.00-	12.50250
Period				· 500020	Board Games - US	25,000,000.00-	18,970,000.00-	6,030,000.00	24.12000-
Profit Cent				· 500030	Card Games - US	37,500,000.00-	21,540,000.00-	15,960,000.00	42.56000-
Partner PC				· 500060	Distribution Center	0.00	9,165,500.00-	9,165,500.00-	x/o
Company Code									

Figure 7.5: Drilldown on account to see profit center detail

There are also some interesting buttons that you can use. Most are fairly self-explanatory, but here are three most used. The 🔳 button allows you to call additional reports (see Figure 7.6).

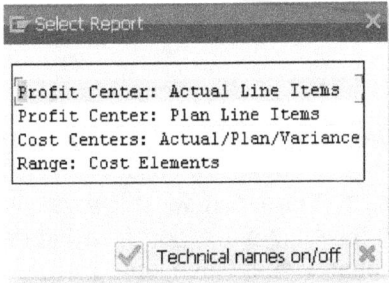

Figure 7.6: Call additional reports

Another useful button is 📝 which allows you to format sections of the report to show exceptions to predefined rules or variance values. For example, you may want to format the variance percentage column to highlight exceptions for easier visibility and analysis. You would select the column and click on the exception button to create the exception rule (see Figure 7.7). Here, you can define the lower and upper threshold values and how you want the exception to display on the report (see Figure 7.8).

Exception	1	Variance					
Area of validity							
Column							
% variance							
Status							
Exception 1 already exists							
Lower threshold				Upper threshold			
✓ Active				✓ Active			
Threshold	15.000-			Threshold	10.000		
Display in	1			Display in	1		
Color below threshold		Condition		Color above threshold		Condition	
○ Green	○○●	● Less than	◁	● Green	○○●	● Greater than/equal to	▷
● Red	●○○	○ Less than/equal to	◁	○ Red	●○○	○ Greater than	▷

Figure 7.7: Create an exception for a column

155

Profit Center		Plan	Actual	Variance	Var. %
˅ 5000	Smarter Sisters	102,500,000.00-	94,676,500.00-	7,823,500.00	7.63268-
• 500010	Video Games - US	40,000,000.00-	45,001,000.00-	5,001,000.00-	12.50250
• 500020	Board Games - US	25,000,000.00-	18,970,000.00-	6,030,000.00	24.12000-
• 500030	Card Games - US	37,500,000.00-	21,540,000.00-	15,960,000.00	42.56000-
• 500060	Distribution Center	0.00	9,165,500.00-	9,165,500.00-	x/0

Figure 7.8: Report showing exceptions

The last button to try is 🖹, which allows you to export the report into either an SAP object list or a spreadsheet. Because the drilldown report is made up of a number of characteristics, the export will allow you to select which characteristics you want to have in your export (see Figure 7.9) and then will present them in the chosen format (see Figure 7.10).

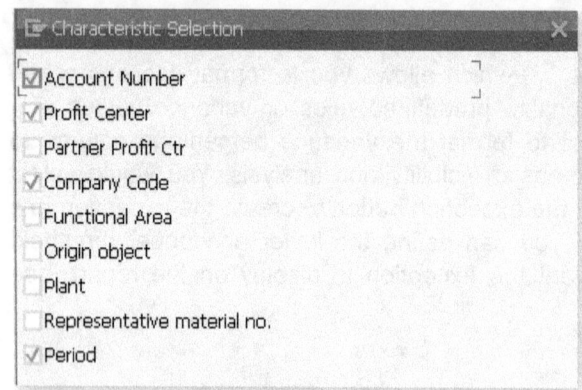

Figure 7.9: Characteristics selected for export

	A	B	C	D	E	F	G	H
1					Plan	Actual	Variance	Var. %
2	Account Number	Profit Center	Company Code	Period	1 USD	1 USD	1 USD	1
3	410000 Sales Revenue	500010 Video Games - US	7000 Smarter Sisters US	January	-20,000,000.00	0.00	20,000,000.00	-100.00
4	410000 Sales Revenue	500010 Video Games - US	7000 Smarter Sisters US	February	-20,000,000.00	-45,001,000.00	-25,001,000.00	125.01
5	410000 Sales Revenue	500020 Board Games - US	7000 Smarter Sisters US	January	-12,500,000.00	0.00	12,500,000.00	-100.00
6	410000 Sales Revenue	500020 Board Games - US	7000 Smarter Sisters US	February	-12,500,000.00	-18,970,000.00	-6,470,000.00	51.76
7	410000 Sales Revenue	500030 Card Games - US	7000 Smarter Sisters US	January	-18,750,000.00	0.00	18,750,000.00	-100.00
8	410000 Sales Revenue	500030 Card Games - US	7000 Smarter Sisters US	February	-18,750,000.00	-21,540,000.00	-2,790,000.00	14.88
9	410000 Sales Revenue	500060 Distribution Center	7000 Smarter Sisters US	January	0.00	0.00	0.00	0.00
10	410000 Sales Revenue	500060 Distribution Center	7000 Smarter Sisters US	February	0.00	-9,165,500.00	-9,165,500.00	0.00

Figure 7.10: Report exported to Excel

The LIST ORIENTED REPORTS menu offers some additional reporting options (one example will be shown):

- ▶ S_ALR_87009712 – Profit Center List:
  Plan/Actual—This is a plan actual variance report that is summarized by profit center. Reports such as this, with lists in the de-

scription, generally do not have account-level detail and only show overall values for the object.

- S_ALR_87013340 – Profit Center Group:
  Plan/Actual/Variance—This presents similar information to the first report that you saw in the INTERACTIVE REPORTING section.
- S_ALR_87009726 – Profit Center Group:
  Plan/Actual/Variance by Origin—This has a similar layout to the previous report, but subtotals the data by origin object such as cost center, production order, internal order, etc.
- S_ALR_87009734 – Profit Center Group:
  Plan/Plan/Variance—This is similar to interactive report S_ALR_87013330 and allows you to compare two plan versions.
- S_ALR_87009717 – Profit Center Group:
  Quarterly Comparison of Actual Data—This shows a quarterly P&L breakdown for the selected fiscal year.
- S_ALR_87013342 – Profit Center:
  Statistical Key Figures –This compares actual versus plan statistical key figures for profit centers or groups.

The selection screens for list-oriented reports are similar to the interactive reports (see Figure 7.11). However, the output is somewhat different. You do not have the drilldown characteristics as you had in the interactive reports. Here, you only have fixed characteristics such as profit center and account. You also have a VARIATION pane whose values are defined by the profit center group that you enter on the selection screen. Here, you can select any of the values in the VARIATION pane and display the report at that level. When you run a report painter report, you actually run it for the report group that the report is assigned to.

In some cases, there is only one report in a report group, so you will not see the REPORTS pane. If you see a REPORTS pane, then there are multiple reports in the group and you can select between the reports directly in the REPORTS pane. In the case of many of the classic PCA list reports, there will be two reports, one without elimination of internal business volume (EIBV) (see Figure 7.12) and one with elimination of internal business volume. In the case of the transfer pricing scenario, the report without EIBV will show the inter-profit center sales and cost of sales while the other one will not (see Figure 7.13).

Reporting in Profit Center Accounting

Selection values	
Controlling Area	7000
Fiscal Year	2016
From Period	1
To Period	2
Plan Version	0

Selection Groups			
Profit Center Group	5000		
Or value(s)		to	
Profit and Loss Accounts Group	PCA63.99		
Or value(s)		to	
Balance Sheet Account Group	PCA7.99		
Or value(s)		to	

Figure 7.11: Selection for list-oriented report

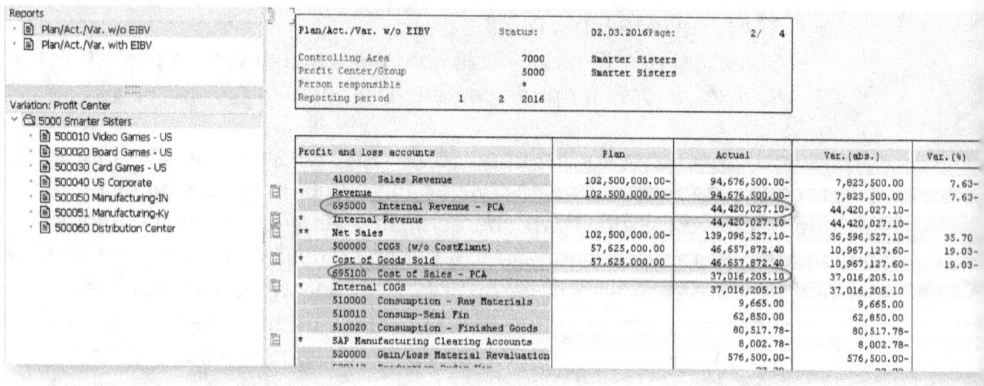

Figure 7.12: List-oriented report without EIBV

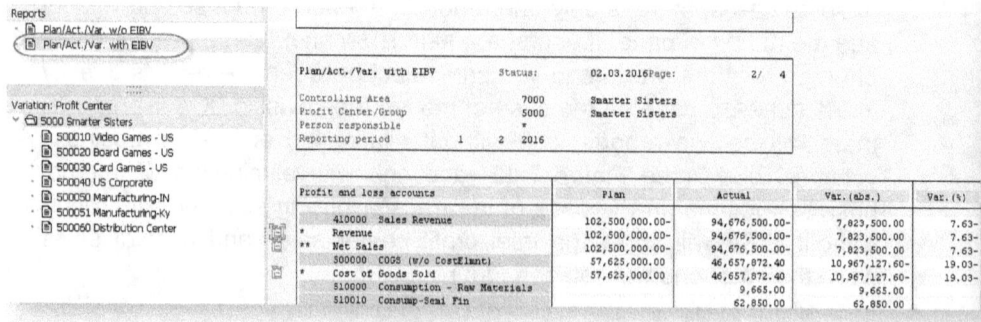

Figure 7.13: List-oriented report with EIBV

158

Within list-oriented reports, you can also use the button to call additional reports and you can use the button to export the report in a variety of formats. You can also use the button to change or activate certain display options. A useful option here is to activate office integration (see Figure 7.14). This opens the report in SAP in an embedded spreadsheet (see Figure 7.15) and then you can use FILE • SAVE AS or F12 to export the report as a local copy.

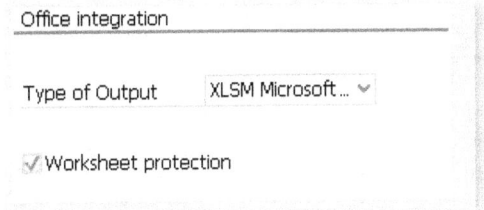

Figure 7.14: Activate office integration for report

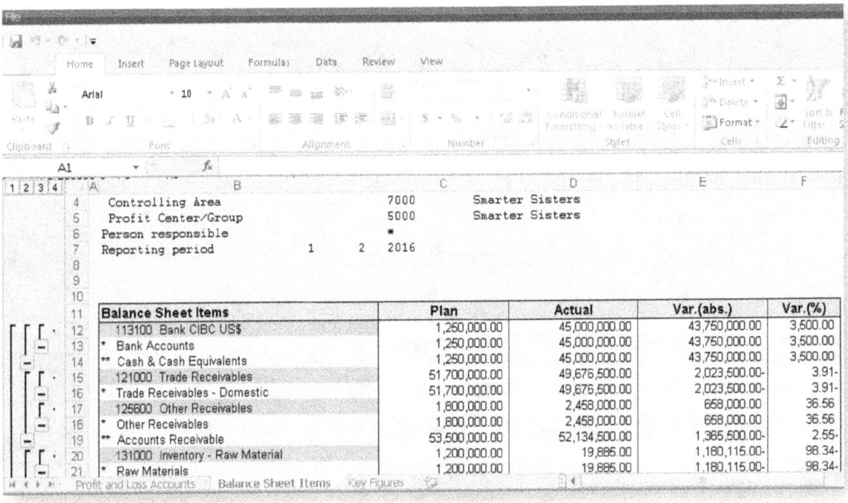

Balance Sheet Items	Plan	Actual	Var.(abs.)	Var.(%)
113100 Bank CIBC US$	1,250,000.00	45,000,000.00	43,750,000.00	3,500.00
* Bank Accounts	1,250,000.00	45,000,000.00	43,750,000.00	3,500.00
** Cash & Cash Equivalents	1,250,000.00	45,000,000.00	43,750,000.00	3,500.00
121000 Trade Receivables	51,700,000.00	49,676,500.00	2,023,500.00-	3.91-
* Trade Receivables - Domestic	51,700,000.00	49,676,500.00	2,023,500.00-	3.91-
125600 Other Receivables	1,800,000.00	2,458,000.00	658,000.00	36.56
* Other Receivables	1,800,000.00	2,458,000.00	658,000.00	36.56
** Accounts Receivable	53,500,000.00	52,134,500.00	1,365,500.00-	2.55-
131000 Inventory - Raw Material	1,200,000.00	19,885.00	1,180,115.00-	98.34-
* Raw Materials	1,200,000.00	19,885.00	1,180,115.00-	98.34-

Figure 7.15: Report with active office integration

You may have noticed that there are no separate reports for key figures or ROI in the list-oriented section of the menu. However, these values are available in some of the list-oriented reports calculated based on your selected P&L and balance sheet account groups (see Figure 7.16).

```
Plan/Act./Var. with EIBV          Status:          02.03.2016

Controlling Area                  7000             Smarter Sisters
Profit Center/Group               5000             Smarter Sisters
Person responsible                *
Reporting period           1      2    2016
```

Key figures	Plan	Actual
Profit	11,083,666.64-	16,543,531.77-
Fixed capital	140,608,761.89	187,034,329.51
Return on investment	7.88-	8.85-

Figure 7.16: ROI in a list-oriented report

The third folder in the information systems menu is the LINE ITEM REPORTS. Here, you can run line item reports for actual values (KE5Z) and for planned values (KE5Y). There are also reports for profit center payables and receivables which can be expanded to show open items (Figure 7.17) and which will allow drilldown to the original FI document.

```
Profit Center: Payables

Variation: Profit Center
  5000 Smarter Sisters       Profit Center: Payables       Date: 02.03.2016    Page: 2 / 2
    500010 Video Games - US
    500020 Board Games - US  Company Code         5000      Smarter Sisters US
    500030 Card Games - US   Profit Center Group  5000      Smarter Sisters
    500040 US Corporate      Posting date:        29.02.2016
    500050 Manufacturing
                             Documents: Company code currency   Accounts Payab  Valuation diff   Total

                             *   100025  National Cardboard         12,000.00-                    12,000.00-
                             *   100026  Countex Wright Auditors    17,000.00-                    17,000.00-
                             *   100027  Fancy Extruders            18,750.00-                    18,750.00-
                                 5105600823  5105600823             45,000.00-                    45,000.00-
                                 5105600826  5105600826              8,000.00-                     8,000.00-
                                 5105600828  5105600828             35,000.00-                    35,000.00-
                             *   100029  Nice and Glossy Printers   88,000.00-                    88,000.00-
                             *   100030  Global Plastic Products    10,687.02-                    10,687.02-
                             *   100031  Counter feet printers      52,482.27-                    52,482.27-
                             *   100032  Massive Plastic Formers    35,000.00-                    35,000.00-
                             *   100033  Mr sell o fane             10,000.00-                    10,000.00-
                             **  211000  Trade Payables            243,919.29-                   243,919.29-
                             *** Total                             243,919.29-                   243,919.29-
```

Figure 7.17: PCA payables report

Finally, there are some reports that allow you to display any balance sheet items that have been transferred periodically. The most useful of these are for customers and vendors since those are the only two items where it is required to perform periodic transfer.

The final folder in the profit center accounting information system is called SPECIAL FUNCTIONS and contains several useful reports. The option PROFIT CENTER: TOTALS RECORDS, also accessed by transaction code

2KEE, gives a view into the PCA totals table and can be a very useful report for displaying plan and/or actual total values for profit centers. The menu option PROFIT CENTER: MASTER DATA INDEX accessed with transaction KE5X provides a profit center master data listing.

7.2 Profit center reporting in the new GL

With profit center accounting being incorporated into the GL, much of the reporting for profit centers now falls under the information system menu for the GL (see Figure 7.18).

Figure 7.18: General ledger information system menu

There is a specific folder for REPORTS FOR PROFIT CENTER ACCOUNTING and there are also some profit center-related reports in the LINE ITEMS folder. The reports in the REPORTS FOR PROFIT CENTER ACCOUNTING folder are interactive drilldown reports similar to the interactive reports that you saw in the classic PCA. Not all the reports in PCA are available, but you have the following:

- ▶ S_E38_98000088 – Profit Center Group:
  Plan/Actual/Variance—This gives a plan/actual variance report similar to classic PCA report S_ALR_87013326.
- ▶ S_E38_98000089 – Profit Center Group:
  Plan/Plan/Actual—This gives a plan actual variance report and allows you to select two different plan versions similar to classic PCA report S_ALR_87013330.

161

- S_E38_98000090 – Profit Center Group:
  Key Figures—This allows you to display the plan versus actual values for a selected fiscal year plan version, profit center, or group, and financial statement version for profit, fixed capital, and profit adjusted for cost of capital (based on an entered rate) and return on investment (ROI).

- S_E38_98000091 – Profit Center Comparison:
  ROI—This allows you to compare the actual and planned ROI between two selected profit centers based on selected P&L and balance sheet items from the financial statement version.

The selection parameters are different for the GL-based reports. In addition to a range of GENERAL SELECTION options such as currency type, company code, and account, there is also the REPORT SELECTION section (see Figure 7.19). Here, instead of the account group, you need to have a financial statement version to define the structure of the output, but the profit center group is still relevant. There is also a selection for OUTPUT TYPE which defines the way the report will appear. The option `graphical report output` gives an output close to the interactive display that you saw in the classic PCA interactive reports (see Figure 7.20). The `classic drilldown report` outputs the report in the old-school SAP drilldown format. Finally, the `object list` gives an object list output directly in an ALV grid format. You can still achieve this later from within the graphical report by clicking on the 📄 button and selecting the object list option.

Report selections			
Ledger	0L	IFRS Ledger	
Controlling Area	7000	Smarter Sisters	
FIS Annual Rep.Struc	5000	SAP Best Practices Finan...	
Plan Version	0	Plan/actual version	
Fiscal year	2016	2016	
From period	1	January	
To period	2	February	
Profit Center Group	5000		
Or values		to	

Parameters for Special Evaluations
☐ Alternative Account Number

Output type
◉ Graphical report output
◯ Classic drilldown report
◯ Object list (more than one lead column)

Figure 7.19: Selection for S_E38_98000088 report

REPORTING IN PROFIT CENTER ACCOUNTING

Navigation	P	N	Text	FS Item/Account	Plan	Actual	Variance	Var. %
⌄ Currency Type				⌄ Financial Statement Version	0.00	0.00	0.00	x/o
• 10			Company ...	⌄ Profit and Loss Statement	202,916,333.28	20,504,460.27-	223,420,793.55-	110.10488-
⌄ Currency				⌄ Net Income After Taxes	202,916,333.28	20,504,460.27-	223,420,793.55-	110.10488-
• USD			US Dollar	⌄ Income Before Taxes	202,916,333.28	20,504,460.27-	223,420,793.55-	110.10488-
• FS Item/Ac				⌄ Operating Profit	202,916,333.28	20,504,460.27-	223,420,793.55-	110.10488-
• Account Numb				⌄ Gross Profit	169,125,000.00	52,596,581.40-	221,721,581.40-	131.09924-
• Cost Element				⌄ Net Sales	102,500,000.00	94,676,500.00-	197,176,500.00-	192.36732-
• Segment				⌄ Revenue	102,500,000.00	94,676,500.00-	197,176,500.00-	192.36732-
• Profit Center				• Sales Reve	102,500,000.00	94,676,500.00-	197,176,500.00-	192.36732-
• Partner PC				> Internal Reven	0.00	0.00	0.00	x/o
• Business Area				> Cost of Goods Sol	66,625,000.00	42,079,918.60	24,545,081.40-	36.84065-
• Functional Are				⌄ Operating Expenses	33,791,333.28	32,092,121.13	1,699,212.15-	5.02854-
• Company Code				> Personnel Expens	10,786,666.68	10,616,799.62	169,867.06-	1.57479-
				> Utilities	1,653,333.36	1,614,898.00	38,435.36-	2.32472-
				> Amortization	1,266,666.66	1,294,888.89	28,222.23	2.22807
				> Advertising, Office	20,084,666.58	18,565,534.62	1,519,131.96-	7.56364-
				> Miscellaneous	0.00	0.00	0.00	x/o
				> FI-CO Reconciliatio	0.00	0.00	0.00	x/o

Figure 7.20: Output for S_E38_98000088 report

As mentioned, there are some profit center-related reports under the LINE ITEMS menu in the information system (see Figure 7.21). Here, you can find drilldown reports for receivables and payables by profit center. They both work in the same way, so only the payables report is shown as an example (see Figure 7.22). As these are drilldown reports, you can display details by any of the characteristics available in the NAVIGATION pane, such as details by vendor or document.

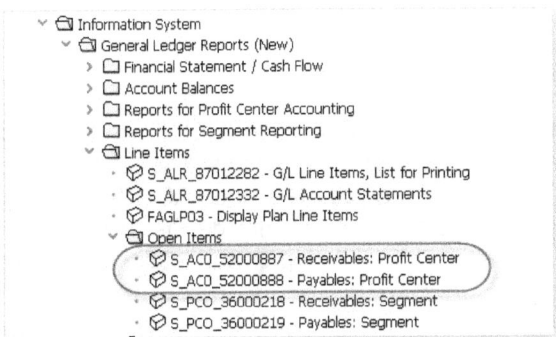

Figure 7.21: Profit center receivables and payables reports

Payables: Profit Center							
Navigation	P	N	Text	Profit Center			Payables in LC
• Local Currency				• 500010	Video Games - US		82,418.00-
• Document Nur				• 500020	Board Games - US		133,981.44-
• Company Code				• 500030	Card Games - US		110,944.00-
• Fiscal Year				• 500040	US Corporate		216,053.98-
• Line item				• 500050	Manufacturing		89,358.00-
• G/L				• Result			632,755.42-
• Vendor							
• Profit Center							

Figure 7.22: GL payables by profit center

163

You saw earlier that you can create an object list or spreadsheet output from the interactive list by clicking on the 🗔 button and selecting the type of output and restricting the characteristic selection. With a little formatting, you can make a useful list showing AP items by profit center (see Figure 7.23).

0SAPPAYABL01	Payables: Profit Center						
Data from	03.03.2016 12:29:43						
Acct Type	K						
Ledger	0L IFRS Ledger						
Profit Center	Year	Itm	G/L Account	Vendor	Document	LCurr	CoCd ∑	Payables in LC
500010	2016	1	0020/211000	100026	1900000000	USD	6000	900.00-
	2016	1	0020/211000	100033	1900000004	USD	6000	52,691.00-
	2016	1	0020/211000	100034	1900000003	USD	6000	28,827.00-
500010 △								82,418.00-
500020	2016	1	0020/211000	100026	1900000000	USD	6000	2,000.00-
	2016	1	0020/211000	100031	1900000002	USD	6000	36,418.44-
	2016	1	0020/211000	100033	1900000004	USD	6000	68,974.00-
	2016	1	0020/211000	100034	1900000003	USD	6000	26,589.00-
500020 △								133,981.44-
500030	2016	1	0020/211000	100026	1900000000	USD	6000	2,100.00-
	2016	1	0020/211000	100033	1900000004	USD	6000	39,874.00-
	2016	1	0020/211000	100034	1900000003	USD	6000	68,970.00-
500030 △								110,944.00-
500040	2016	1	0020/211000	100026	1900000005	USD	6000	100,000.00-
	2016	1	0020/211000	100031	1900000002	USD	6000	31,382.98-
	2016	1	0020/211000	100033	1900000004	USD	6000	48,974.00-
	2016	1	0020/211000	100034	1900000003	USD	6000	35,697.00-
500040 △								216,053.98-
500050	2016	1	0020/211000	100026	1900000005	USD	6000	25,000.00-
	2016	1	0020/211000	100033	1900000004	USD	6000	58,461.00-
	2016	1	0020/211000	100034	1900000003	USD	6000	5,897.00-
500050 △								89,358.00-
△							**	632,755.42-

Figure 7.23: Profit center payables object list view

With profit center accounting being incorporated into the GL, there are no separate line item reports associated with profit centers. The standard GL line item reports, such as FAGLL03 for actual data and FAGLP03 for plan data, should be used. Simply create layouts to include the profit center field (see Figure 7.24) and then use it for filtering or sub-totaling as required.

G/L Account	"								
Company Code	6000								
Ledger	0L								
S	Assignment	Documen	BusA	Ty	Doc. Date	PK ∑	Amount in local cur.	LCurr	Profit Center	Segment
✓	20160221	4900000001		WA	21.02.2016	81	6,968.64	USD	500050	3000
						*	6,968.64	USD		
Account 510000					△ **		6,968.64	USD		
✓	20160221	4900000001		WA	21.02.2016	81	62,500.00	USD	500050	3000
						*	62,500.00	USD		
Account 510010					△ **		62,500.00	USD		
✓	20160221	4900000000		WA	21.02.2016	91	33,217.50-	USD	500050	3000
						*	33,217.50-	USD		
Account 510020					△ **		33,217.50-	USD		
✓	1000007	100000001		AB	21.02.2016	50	40,261.14-	USD	500050	3000
						*	40,261.14-	USD		
Account 539999					△ **		40,261.14-	USD		

Figure 7.24: GL actual line items with profit center

Several of the other standard GL reports can also be run using a profit center in the selection criteria to give profit center-specific reports. Some of the more common reports that can be run by profit center include:

- S_PL0_86000028 – Financial Statement: Actual/Actual Comparison
- S_ALR_87012284 – Financial Statement
- S_EBS_44000137 – Financial Statement: Ledger Comparison
- S_PL0_86000029 – Financial Statement: Plan/Actual Comparison
- S_ALR_87012277 – GL Account Balances
- S_PL0_86000030 – GL Account Balances (New)
- S_PL0_86000031 – Transaction Figures: Account Balance
- S_ALR_87012301 – Totals and Balances
- S_PL0_86000032 – Structured Account Balances

Within some of the above reports, you see the profit center directly on the selection screen, on others you may have to use the dynamic selection button to find the profit center field.

7.3 Report painter and drilldown options

SAP provides a number of tools to allow you to create your own reports. Sometimes, if the reporting requirement is particularly complex, you have to have a developer build a report. In other cases, especially in finance and controlling, you may be able to use the tools which are provided to build your own reports. Among the reporting tools that are made available are two which SAP feels could be used by experienced users and not necessarily require technical or functional consulting assistance. You have seen reports built with these tools already in both the classic PCA and the new GL; these are report painter and drilldown reporting.

Look at the report painter tool. The basic structure of report painter is shown in Figure 7.25.

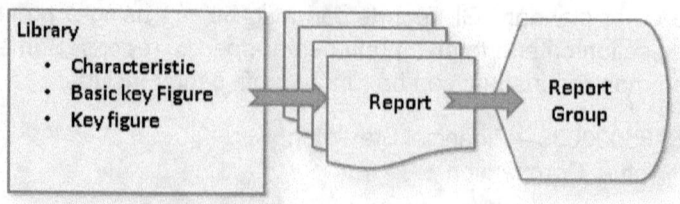

Figure 7.25: Report painter structure

All report painter reports are created with reference to a *library*. There are many predefined libraries in SAP and it is also possible to create libraries, although that is beyond the scope of this book. The library is a collection of *characteristics*, *basic key figures*, and *key figures* contained in a reporting table. The characteristic is a non-numeric value that you can use in your report such as an account or a profit center. The basic key figure is a numeric value field, such as an amount in local currency or quantity. The key figure is a predefined combination of a basic key figure and one or more characteristics such as actual costs in the current period.

Once the reports have been created, they need to be assigned to a report group before you can run them. Sometimes there is only one report assigned to a report group, other times there are multiple reports in a group, as shown in Figure 7.12, with the EBIV options. In the report group, you can also define drilldowns from your report into other reports through functionality called *report to report interface* which allows you to assign other reports to call or drill into from your report painter report.

For the classic PCA, the delivered libraries all start with 8A and are shown in Figure 7.26. You can view these in transaction GRR3. The libraries are represented by the folders, and the reports associated with the libraries can be found by opening the folders. You can display libraries in transaction GR23 and see what characteristics, basic key figures, and key figures are contained within a library (see Figure 7.27).

8A0	EC-PCA: Standard Reports	SAP
8A1	EC-PCA: Standard Reports Rel. 2.1	SAP
8A2	EC-PCA: Standard Reports	JPRINGLE
8A3	EC-PCA: Line Item Reports	SAP
8A4	EC-PCA: Drilldown, Open Items	SAP
8A4-0010	Receivables	SAP
8A4-0012	Payables	SAP
8A5	EC-PCA: Average Balance Reports	JPRINGLE
8AW	Profit Center - Workplace Reports	SAP

Figure 7.26: Classic PCA report libraries

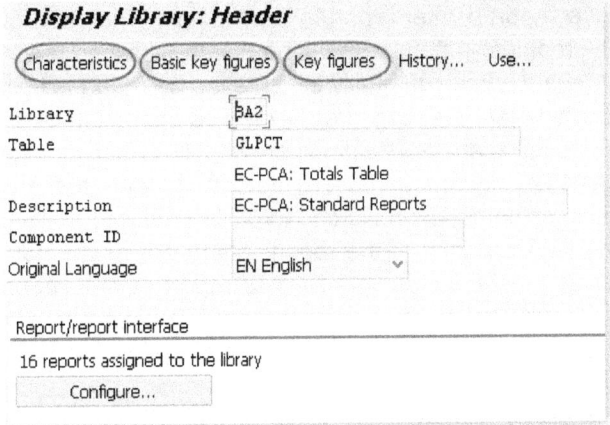

Figure 7.27: Library for standard PCA reports

By clicking on the outlined buttons shown in Figure 7.27, you can display the components of the library. As an example, you can see some of the characteristics in library 8A2 shown in Figure 7.28. The check box on the left of the NAME indicates that the component can be used in reports for this library.

Library	8A2		
Table	GLPCT	EC-PCA: Totals Table	
Description	EC-PCA: Standard Reports		

Characteristics			
Name	Default set	Short text	Pos
RLDNR	00008A-RLDN...	Ledger	1
KOKRS	00008A-KOKR...	Controlling Area	2
RBUKRS		Company Code	3
RPRCTR		Profit Center	4
RACCT		Account Number	5
RYEAR	00008A-RYEA...	Fiscal Year	6
RPMAX	00008A-RPMA...	Period	7
RVERS		Version	8
SPRCTR		Partner Profit Center	9
EPRCTR		Partner profit center for elimination of internal	10
RRCTY		Record Type	11

Figure 7.28: Characteristics in library 8A2

For the new GL, the report libraries are 0FL – NEW GENERAL LEDGER and 0FS – FI-GL (NEW): TOTALS AND STATKEYFIGS.

167

The basic building of a report painter report is fairly simple. The view for building the report is graphical in nature, meaning that the finished report will resemble that structure when you finally execute it. The report is built using rows and columns where the rows are based on a characteristic or combination of characteristics and the columns are usually a combination of characteristics, basic key figures, and/or key figures. Beyond that, it is possible to add formula columns and rows and to enhance the formatting of the rows, columns, and sections of the report. There are many more advanced features that can be incorporated into a report painter report that are not described here, but you can explore them if you are interested in creating your own reports in SAP.

The transactions for creating or changing report painter reports are GRR1 and GRR2. The report in Figure 5.45 was created in report painter and the editing view of that report can be seen in Figure 7.29.

Report	ZSKF	GL-SKF Report			
Section	0001				
Standard layout	SAP				
Format group:	1	1	1		0
Statistical Key Figures	Actual	Plan	Var.(abs)		Var.(%)
* All values	XXX,XXX,XXX.XX	XXX,XXX,XXX.XX	XXX,XXX,XXX.XX		XXX,XXX,XXX
** Total	XXX,XXX,XXX.XX	XXX,XXX,XXX.XX	XXX,XXX,XXX.XX		XXX,XXX,XXX

Figure 7.29: Creating a report painter report

Once you build your report painter reports and assign them to report groups, you can either run them from the transaction GR55 or, even better, have a custom transaction code assigned to the report group so that access can be more easily controlled through security.

The other tool used to create reports is drilldown reporting. This is available in the classic PCA and the new GL, but is accessed under different sets of transaction codes in each area. The basic structure of how drilldown reporting works is shown in Figure 7.30.

In the classic PCA, there are essentially two types of drilldown reports, the *basic report* and the *form-based report*. The basic report is easy to define and simply requires you to pick the characteristics, key figures, and variables to report on. The report based on a form is more structured and requires that you build a *form* that defines the report layout prior to defining the report. In the new GL, there is no option to create basic reports, so all drilldown reports are based on a form. Building the form is very similar to building a report painter report and is shown a little later.

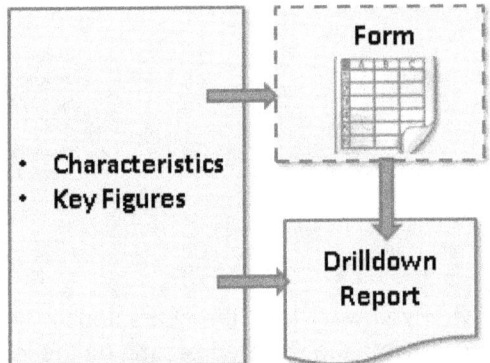

Figure 7.30: Basic structure of drilldown reporting

To create the basic report or a form-based report in classic PCA, you can use transaction KE81 (see Figure 7.31).

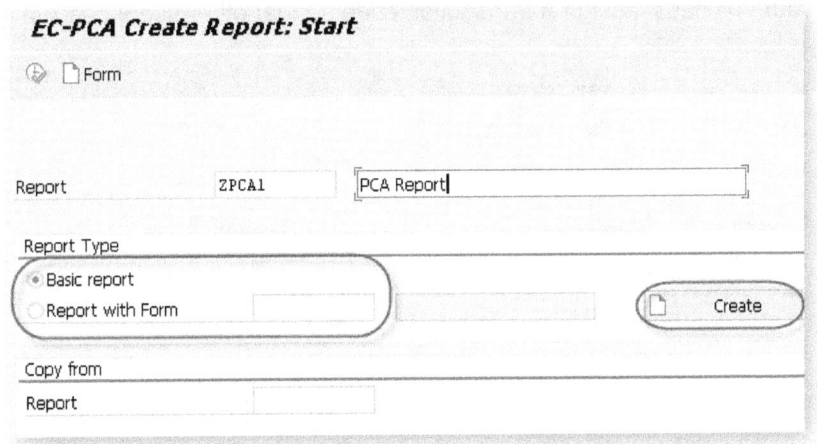

Figure 7.31: Initial screen classic PCA drilldown report

Initially, you have the option to choose whether you are going to create a BASIC REPORT or a REPORT WITH FORM. Once you have pressed the Create button, you can define the characteristics, key figures, and variables for your report.

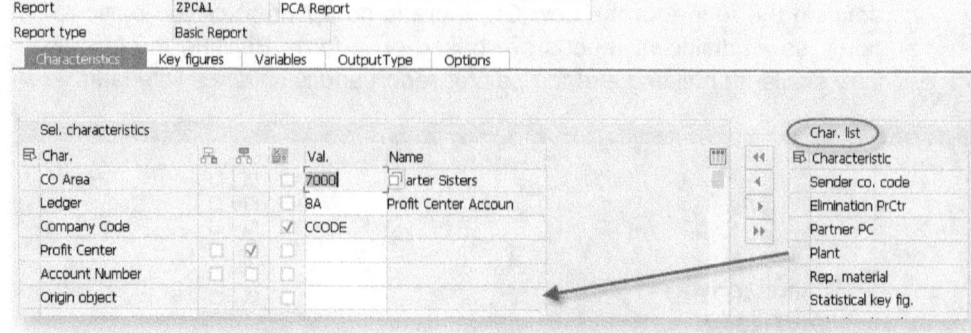

Figure 7.32: Select characteristics

For characteristics, you select what you want from the characteristic list on the right of the screen and move it into the selected section on the left (see Figure 7.32). Follow a similar process with the key figures (see Figure 7.33). The VARIABLES tab is where you define the values on the initial selection screen when you run the report. The OUTPUT TYPE tab allows you to define how the report is presented and the OPTIONS tab gives some printing and other options. Once you have created a report to use in your business, assign a transaction code so that other users can run it (see Figure 7.34.).

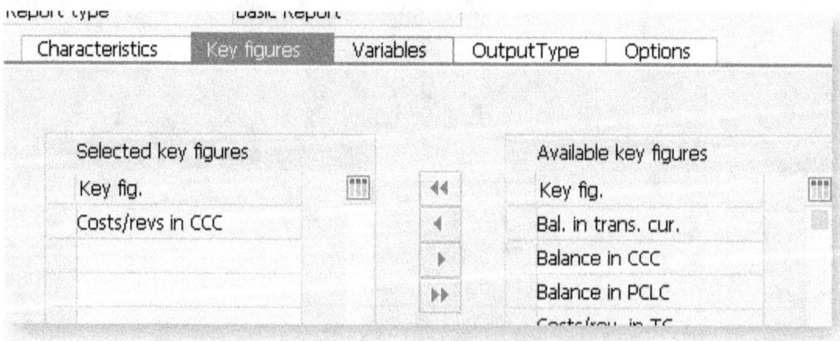

Figure 7.33: Select key figures

When you run the report, you see the characteristics you specified (in Figure 7.32) in the navigation window (see Figure 7.35).

You can also create form-based reports in the classic PCA by either using an existing form or creating your own form in transaction KE84. As mentioned for new GL drilldown reports, it is necessary to have a form. Form creation for the new GL is shown since the mechanics are similar for the forms in classic PCA.

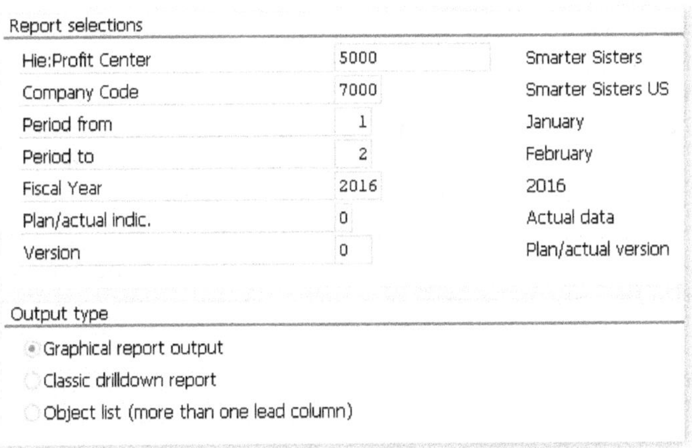

Report selections		
Hie:Profit Center	5000	Smarter Sisters
Company Code	7000	Smarter Sisters US
Period from	1	January
Period to	2	February
Fiscal Year	2016	2016
Plan/actual indic.	0	Actual data
Version	0	Plan/actual version

Output type
- ● Graphical report output
- ○ Classic drilldown report
- ○ Object list (more than one lead column)

Figure 7.34: Selection screen for created drilldown report

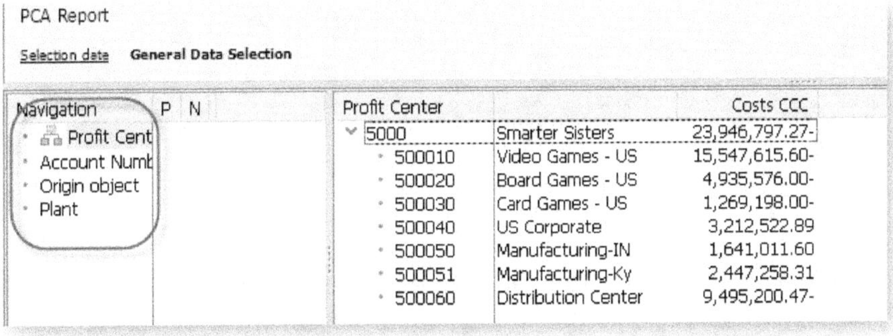

PCA Report

Selection date General Data Selection

Navigation	P	N	Profit Center		Costs CCC
🔹 Profit Cent			⌄ 5000	Smarter Sisters	23,946,797.27-
• Account Numb			• 500010	Video Games - US	15,547,615.60-
• Origin object			• 500020	Board Games - US	4,935,576.00-
• Plant			• 500030	Card Games - US	1,269,198.00-
			• 500040	US Corporate	3,212,522.89
			• 500050	Manufacturing-IN	1,641,011.60
			• 500051	Manufacturing-Ky	2,447,258.31
			• 500060	Distribution Center	9,495,200.47-

Figure 7.35: User-defined drilldown report

In the new GL, you can create a form using transaction FGI4 (see Figure 7.36).

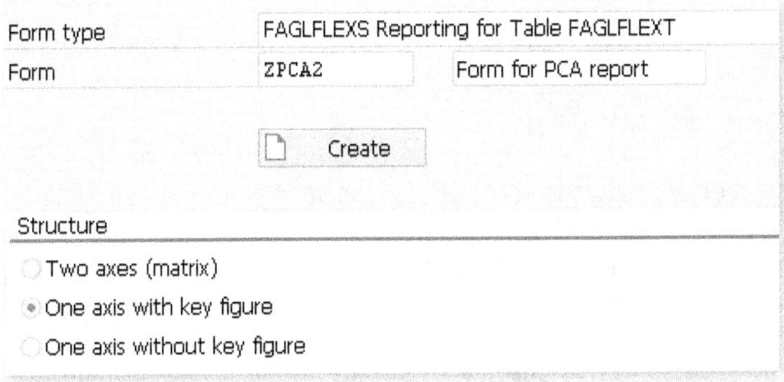

Form type	FAGLFLEXS Reporting for Table FAGLFLEXT	
Form	ZPCA2	Form for PCA report

        📄 Create

Structure
- ○ Two axes (matrix)
- ● One axis with key figure
- ○ One axis without key figure

Figure 7.36: Create form for drilldown report

For a new GL form, you need to select a FORM TYPE which defines the table and fields available in the form. In classic PCA, there is no form type, but all other steps are similar. There are form types for GL reporting from FAGLFLEXT as well as for payables and receivables for profit centers and segments. You pick the STRUCTURE to define how the form layout will appear. Finally, you can copy from an existing form. When you create the form, the appearance is defined by the STRUCTURE option you selected on the previous screen. The form is a report painter object and can be edited and formatted like any other report painter report (see Figure 7.37).

Form	ZPCA2	Form for PCA report
Key Figure		
Plan &1FY &1PF-&1PT	XXX,XXX,XXX	
Act. &1FY &1PF-&1PT	XXX,XXX,XXX	
Variance	XXX,XXX,XXX	
% Variance	XXX,XXX,XXX	

Figure 7.37: Create form for drilldown reporting

After creating the form, you can create the report using transaction FGI1 (KE81 in classic PCA). The initial screen is shown in Figure 7.38.

Report type	FAGLFLEXS Reporting for Table FAGLFLEXT
Report	ZPCA2 — PCA Report
With form	ZPCA2 — Form for PCA report

Figure 7.38: Create drilldown report

In the next step of creating the form-based report, select the CHARACTERISTICS (see Figure 7.39) and set up the VARIABLES, OUTPUT TYPE, and OPTIONS similar to the basic report. Note that in this case, you don't have to define key figures because you have defined them in the form.

You have only scratched the surface of what can be achieved using report painter and/or drilldown reporting. There are many features and techniques that aren't addressed here, but I hope that I have given an idea of what can be achieved using these tools.

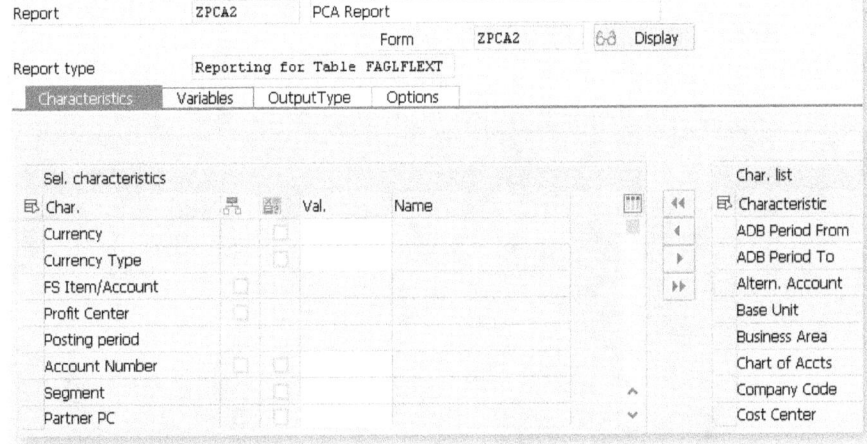

Figure 7.39: FGI1 characteristics

Navigation	P	N	Text	FS Item/Account	Plan	Actual	Variance	Var. %
˅ Currency				· Accumulated Depreciation -	15,098,334.00-	12,765,000.00-	2,333,334.00	15.45425-
· USD			US Dollar	· Accumulated Depreciation -	588,333.00-	1,516,666.67-	928,333.67-	157.79051
˅ Currency Type				· Accumulated Depreciation -	466,668.00-	2,000,000.00-	1,533,332.00-	328.57020
· 10			Company code	· Accumulated Depreciation -	402,000.00-	1,116,000.00-	714,000.00-	177.61194
· FS Item/Accou				· Accumulated Depreciation -	24,000.00-	156,000.00-	132,000.00-	550.00000
· Profit Center				· Accumulated Depreciation -	4,051,906.00-	5,061,222.22-	1,009,316.22-	24.90967
· Posting period				· Accumulated Depreciation -	450,000.00-	956,000.00-	506,000.00-	112.44444
· Account Numb				· Advertising	900,000.00	905,928.00	5,928.00	0.65867
· Segment				· Audit fees	100,000.00	100,000.00	0.00	0.00000
· Partner PC				· Bank CIBC US$	1,250,000.00	0.00	1,250,000.00	100.00000-

Figure 7.40: User-created form-based drilldown report

7.4 Summary

In this chapter, you learned about some of the standard reporting options in both classic PCA and the new GL. You saw that there are a number of standard reports in both modules that can address basic profitability reporting requirements. You learned about the basic structures behind the report painter and the drilldown reporting tools and saw how reports can be created in both the classic PCA and the new GL using each of those tools.

173

You have finished the book.

Sign up for our newsletter!

Want to learn more about new e-books?

Get exclusive free downloads and SAP tips.

Sign up for our newsletter!

Please visit us at *newsletter.espresso-tutorials.com* to find out more.

A The Author

John Pringle is the SAP FICO Competency Group Lead with Illumiti, an SAP Partner and a leading SAP systems integration and management consulting company based in Toronto, Canada. He is the product owner for the SAP all-in-one Mining Solution, one of Illumiti's all-in-one SAP solutions. John has been working in SAP consulting for over 15 years and has previously worked for PwC, IBM and Accenture. He has implemented SAP solutions in a number of industries including mining, automotive, food processing, semi-conductor manufacturing, and industrial and building products.

He is SAP certified in CO and is experienced in implementing most areas within SAP FICO as well as areas in PS, MM, SD and PP. Prior to his consulting career John worked in a variety of business and accounting roles for over 10 years and has also been part of the client team in several large system implementations giving him a unique perspective on the issues faced by both consultants and the business. John has an MBA in Finance and International Business from Schulich School of Business in Toronto and is a CMA and CPA.

B Index

A

Access sequence 141
Activate plan integration for secondary cost elements 97
Activities 67
Activity-Based Costing 46
Actual SKF postings – Settings 132
Alternative hierarchies 34
Assessment 69

B

Balance sheet adjustment 116
Business process 46

C

Classic PCA 17
   Accounts 37
   Activation 17
   Balance Sheet Accounts 110
   Balance Sheet Planning 80
   Copy Planned Data 83
   Flow of actual data 109
   P&L accounts 110
   Plan Allocations 82
   Plan Balance Carryforward 82
Constant for unassigned processes 126
COPA
   Costing based 13
   Purpose of 12
   Revenue Planning 60
   Valuation 14
Costing run 142
Costing type 143
Costing variant 142
Costing versions 145

D

Depreciation and interest simulation 70
Distribution 69
Distribution key 80
Document splitting 125
Drilldown reporting 168
   Basic Report 168
   Form Based 168
Dummy profit center 30

E

Entry view 129

F

FIN_PCA 18
FIN_SEGM 26
Formula planning 84

G

General ledger view 129
Generic file 76
GL Plan Copy 106
Group valuation 137

I

Integrated excel planning – Steps 75
Interactive reporting 152

L

Ledger concept 90
Legal valuation 137
List-oriented reports 152

Index

M
Mandatory field 126

N
New GL PCA 17
    Accounts 37
    Balance Sheet Planning 103
    Benefits 20
    Migration 19
    Planned CO allocations 95
    Planning Layouts 98
    SAP recomendations 19
    Scenarios 18
    Versions 90

O
Online transfer of data to PCA 64

P
Plan Integrated Order 66
Plan Integration-Projects 66
Plan versions 59
Planned allocations 67
Planner profile 73
Planning layout 73
Pricing procedure 141
Profit Center
    Activate 30
    Business defintion 15
    Company code assignment 29
    Numbering 22
Profit Center Accounting
    Possible situations 18
    Purpose of 12
Profit Center Assignment
    Business Process 46
    Cost Center 43
    Fixed Assets 52
    Internal Order 44
    Material Master 47
    Plant Maintenance 52
    Production Order 49
    Project Systems 45
    Repetitive Mfg 50
    Sales Order 50
    Through substitution 50
Profit center standard hierarchy 31
Profit center valuation 138

R
Reference variant 144
Report Painter
    Basic Structure 165
    Library 166
    Report Group 166

S
S/4HANA 16
Sales order substitution 50
Segment 26
    Change value on profit center 27
Standard costing 142
Statistical Key Figure
    Definition 39
    Fixed value 41
    Totals value 41

T
Templates 84
Transaction 1KE4 – Assignment Monitor 54
Transaction 1KEK – Transfer payables and receivables 117
Transaction 3KEH – Additional BS & P&L Accounts 111
Transaction 7KEX – Upload from excel 77
Transaction 9KE0 – Profit center posting 121

transaction F.50 – P&L Adjustment 120
transaction F.5D – Balance sheet adjustment 116
Transaction GLPLUP – Upload from Excel 102
Transaction KCH1 – Create profit center group 34
Transaction KCH1 – Create standard hierarchy 32
Transaction KCH5N – Change standard hierarchy 32
Transaction KDH1 – Create account groups 38
Transaction KE1V – Trasfer plan data from COPA 61
transaction KE1Z – Transfer COPA Plan to GL 92
Transaction KE51 – Create Profit Center 22
Transaction KE59 – Dummy Profit Center 31
Transaction KK01 – Create statistical key figure 40
Transfer control 144

V
Variation 157

W
WIP calculation 113

Z
Zero balance 125

C Disclaimer

This publication contains references to the products of SAP SE.

SAP, R/3, SAP NetWeaver, Duet, PartnerEdge, ByDesign, SAP BusinessObjects Explorer, StreamWork, and other SAP products and services mentioned herein as well as their respective logos are trademarks or registered trademarks of SAP SE in Germany and other countries.

Business Objects and the Business Objects logo, BusinessObjects, Crystal Reports, Crystal Decisions, Web Intelligence, Xcelsius, and other Business Objects products and services mentioned herein as well as their respective logos are trademarks or registered trademarks of Business Objects Software Ltd. Business Objects is an SAP company.

Sybase and Adaptive Server, iAnywhere, Sybase 365, SQL Anywhere, and other Sybase products and services mentioned herein as well as their respective logos are trademarks or registered trademarks of Sybase, Inc. Sybase is an SAP company.

SAP SE is neither the author nor the publisher of this publication and is not responsible for its content. SAP Group shall not be liable for errors or omissions with respect to the materials. The only warranties for SAP Group products and services are those that are set forth in the express warranty statements accompanying such products and services, if any. Nothing herein should be construed as constituting an additional warranty.

More Espresso Tutorials Books

Martin Munzel:

New SAP® Controlling Planning Interface

- ▶ Introduction to Netweaver Business Client
- ▶ Flexible Planning Layouts
- ▶ Plan Data Upload from Excel

http://5011.espresso-tutorials.com

Michael Esser:

Investment Project Controlling with SAP®

- ▶ SAP ERP functionality for investment controlling
- ▶ Concepts, roles and different scenarios
- ▶ Effective planning and reporting

http://5008.espresso-tutorials.com

Stefan Eifler:

Quick Guide to SAP® CO-PA (Profitability Analysis)

- ▶ Basic organizational entities and master data
- ▶ Define the actual value flow
- ▶ Set up a planning environment
- ▶ Create your own reports

http://5018.espresso-tutorials.com

Paul Ovigele:
Reconciling SAP® CO-PA to the General Ledger
- ▶ Learn the Difference between Costing-based and Accounting-based CO-PA
- ▶ Walk through Various Value Flows into CO-PA
- ▶ Match the Cost-of-Sales Account with Corresponding Value Fields in CO-PA

http://5040.espresso-tutorials.com

Tanya Duncan:
Practical Guide to SAP® CO-PC (Product Cost Controlling)
- ▶ Cost Center Planning Process and Costing Run Execution
- ▶ Actual Cost Analysis & Reporting
- ▶ Controlling Master Data
- ▶ Month End Processes in Details

http://5064.espresso-tutorials.com

Ashish Sampat:
First Steps in SAP® Controlling (CO)
- ▶ Cost center and product cost planning and actual cost flow
- ▶ Best practices for cost absorption using Product Cost Controlling
- ▶ Month-end closing activities in SAP Controlling
- ▶ Examples and screenshots based on a case study approach

http://5069.espresso-tutorials.com

Rosana Fonseca:

Practical Guide to SAP® Material Ledger (ML)

- ▶ SAP Material Ledger functionality and key integration points
- ▶ Tips for implementing and using SAP ML effectively
- ▶ The most important SAP Material Ledger reports, including CKM3N
- ▶ Detailed steps for executing a multilevel actual costing run

http://5116.espresso-tutorials.com

www.ingramcontent.com/pod-product-compliance
Lightning Source LLC
Chambersburg PA
CBHW070238190526
45169CB00001B/223